MAKE MONEY YOUR THING!

MAKE MONEY YOUR THING!

DITCH THE SHAME AND DESIGN
YOUR DREAM LIFE

KALEE BOISVERT

TORONTO, 2023

RE:BOOKS

Published in Canada by RE:BOOKS.

ADDRESS:
re:books
380 Macpherson Ave. Suite 306
Toronto ON
M4V 3E3
www.rebooks.ca

First RE: Books Edition: August 2023

ISBN: 978-1-7386702-8-4
eBook ISBN: 978-1-7386702-9-1

Library and Archives upon request.
Title: Make money your thing! : ditch the shame and
design your dream life / Kalee Boisvert.
Names: Boisvert, Kalee, author.
Identifiers: Canadiana (print) 20230177344 | Canadiana (ebook) 20230177352 |
ISBN 9781738670284 (softcover) | ISBN 9781738670291 (EPUB)
Subjects: LCSH: Women—Finance, Personal.
Classification: LCC HG179 .B635 2023 |
DDC 332.0240082—dc23

Printed and bound in Canada.
1 3 5 7 9 10 8 6 4 2

Cover design by: Jordan Lunn
Typesetting by: Karl Hunt

CONTENTS

To Ivy and Jax

INTRODUCTION

WHAT DOES IT MEAN to make money your thing? Great question, and you'll be glad you opened this book to find out. Do any of these sound like your plan for managing your money?

- Yoga, meditation, or some other form of relaxation is required before you check your bank or investment account balances, paired with a glass of wine once you open up your apps.
- A trip to the dentist sounds more appealing than budgeting.
- Your financial plan consists of swiping right on your dating app to land a doctor, lawyer, or Jason Momoa.
- You're a proud member of ten lottery pools. A jackpot is just around the corner.
- You've bought an abundance of books about getting rich that sit collecting dust on your nightstand.

Maybe some of those examples are a tad extreme. But the point is this—do you ever feel like you don't have it all together when it comes to your money, fearing you're doing it all wrong? And maybe you doubt your ability to change this pattern, thinking it requires some sort of money-smarts gene that you didn't inherit.

Please don't give up hope (and read on), because money can be your thing no matter what your bank account balance says. Making money your thing is about moving away from any negative emotions and behaviors that characterize your current relationship with money to create positive change. This book will take you on a journey from avoidance and overwhelm to feeling confident about your money at any stage of life. Money isn't an ultra-complicated concept that's out of your reach. In the chapters that follow, you'll learn the simple, actionable steps you can take so you can feel good about your finances right now, starting exactly where you are.

Perhaps you long to:

- Spend a day pampering yourself guilt-free at a mountain spa you've heard about
- Pay off your credit card debt
- Take your kiddos on a family vacation to Disney
- Watch your savings account steadily grow in value
- Provide your child with financial assistance for college
- Buy the house of your dreams with enough bedrooms for each of your children
- Turn your business idea into reality
- Travel the world
- Quit your job and move to a hot climate

When money is your "thing" you can feel completely at ease about it and confident that you're well on your way to achieving your biggest money dreams. I know this because I made money my thing, and now I get to witness other women do it as well through my work.

If you haven't felt confident about your money up until this point, that's completely understandable. Money is part of your daily life, but there's a good chance you've had zero opportunities in terms of financial literacy. And for that, you can blame your parents (kidding . . . sort of). I'm going to bet that money lessons weren't the focus of dinner conversations in your household. But in your parents' defense, they were probably doing the best they could. They probably weren't taught much about money growing up either.

But surely you've built your financial smarts in school, along with algebra, history, and geography? Again, not likely. Unfortunately, financial literacy still has not been widely adopted in formal education systems in North America. If you didn't have official learning opportunities along the way, it makes sense that you don't feel confident and empowered on the topic of money. Apparently, knowing how to play the recorder, recite the periodic table of elements, and do long division by hand matters more than learning how to earn, save, and invest your money. Sounds ridiculous when you put it that way, doesn't it?

Most adults know nothing about money. And if you think that reaching out to financial experts holds the key to this problem, you may be sadly mistaken. You'll probably find that many major financial institutions are slow to accommodate and welcome women into wealth conversations.

Picture this scenario. A couple walks into a financial advisor's office for the first time. They are escorted into the meeting room to take their seats. In walks Mr. Advisor (and yes, I am saying the advisor is a man for a specific reason; stay with me here). He is dressed in a swanky dark, navy fitted suit, accessorized with a bright red pocket square adding a pop of color. The fresh shine of his shoes is almost blinding. He shakes the couple's hands, introducing himself and thanking them for coming in. He takes his seat at the head of the table and doesn't waste a minute as he dives right into his pitch.

Mr. Advisor maintains direct eye contact with the husband as he boasts about how long he's been in the business. He opens his black folder and takes out his glossy pamphlet, placing it directly in front of the husband as he flips through the pages going into details and explaining his approach. He doesn't break his eye contact. Mr. Advisor is laser-focused on his seemingly private conversation.

The wife moves closer to her husband, trying to get a better view of what's being presented. She looks directly at Mr. Advisor, waiting for him to look at her, waiting for him to make eye contact with her, waiting for him to see her, and waiting to acknowledge her presence. She fidgets in her seat, thinking the shuffle will snap him out of his trance and remind him that she's here and that he is having a meeting with *two* people. Getting annoyed at the complete disregard he has for her existence, she sits forward in her chair and tries to interject with a question. Mr. Advisor doesn't stop; he keeps his focus as he continues to talk to her husband.

Finally, Mr. Advisor pauses for air and asks the husband, "Do you have any questions so far?"

The husband shrugs his shoulders and looks at his wife, "You should probably ask her. She deals with all the money stuff."

Mr. Advisor's face goes as red as his pocket square because he forgot about her.

I added the twist at the end of this story to give it *my* version of a happy ending. Unfortunately, when this scenario plays out in reality, it doesn't usually have a surprise ending with the woman being victorious.

No, the typical meeting continues with Mr. Advisor focusing on the husband and the wife feeling completely left out, wondering why she even made the effort to attend. I've heard it, over and over, from couples who went through almost this exact same scenario, from other women that share stories of what their mothers had gone through, and I witnessed it firsthand early in my career as a team member of male-led advisory businesses.

The financial industry hasn't been a welcoming place for women. In fact, it's been male dominated for far too long. It was designed by men and still caters to them as a result. The language used, how the industry is advertised, how it's presented—it's not focused on the *priorities* of women. The patriarchal undertone that oozes out of this industry has not exactly welcomed women with open arms, encouraging them to be empowered with their money—so it's no wonder why many women don't feel like money can be *their* thing.

And so I was inspired early on to work with women who don't feel fully confident about their financial future. To help all those that fear they "aren't good with money." Money is a vulnerable topic and my goal is that you feel comfortable as you embark on this journey to money confidence, using this book as your guide. It's simple: I want you to make money your thing. And I want you to flourish while you're doing it.

I didn't grow up with money. Being poor was a pervasive theme in my childhood. It impacted so many areas of my life; from living in subsidized housing, to wearing hand-me-downs from my sister with no labels, to dinners of boxed pasta and frozen fish sticks. But I was also an observant introvert, keen on listening and taking in my surroundings. This helped me recognize from an early age the essential role that money played in life. Money was the means to the toys I longed to have as a child, the designer clothes that teenage me desperately wanted, and the key to eliminating my single mom's stress.

I also recognized early on that not everyone seemed to be plagued by the money scarcity that my mom, sister, and I endured. The boys from down the street cruised by in their Powerwheels Jeep; I watched footage from my extended family's world travels and walked through immaculate show homes getting lost in the cavernous rooms. These glimpses of wealth brought me hope. They were the little rays of sunshine that I so desperately needed to have faith that things could be different. That there must be a way out, and I could shed the label of being "poor." I knew it was up to me to make that happen. From a very early age, I set out on a mission to make my own money and achieve my goals.

Each target I hit built up my confidence and belief in myself that anything was possible. That I could succeed at the money game. I started with buying a Super Nintendo, then a pet dog, next my first car, and then my financial goals progressively got bigger, including a post-secondary degree, my first condo, my master's degree, a starter home, then a bigger home, and then accumulating wealth for my financial freedom. It turned out, the circumstances that characterized my childhood didn't define who I was at my core or what I could have or achieve.

Those days were challenging and it would have been easy to give up and give in. I could have turned away from money and hated it for the stress and the struggles that it caused my family. But I chose a different path. I chose to believe that because money was in existence, it was available to everyone.

Including me.

You can be the boss of your money story. And as the master, you can go after exactly what you want. Money can be on your side as your ally. It *can* be your thing.

Remember, I started from *scratch*. And if I was able to make money my thing, then it's possible for everyone. That fueled my drive to share the money confidence I developed with other women.

I wanted to support women, to help them overcome their insecurities around money, and to help them believe in themselves and what they were capable of in their financial lives so that they wouldn't have to go through the stress and struggles that my mom endured.

After finishing my degree I landed a role assisting a financial advisor. I knew this was the right path to supporting women in their financial lives. But several years in, I was still nowhere near the position of my dreams (to *be* the financial advisor). The advisor I worked with failed to take me seriously and treated me more like a personal assistant. My goal to inspire money confidence in women was reignited when I went on maternity leave after having my daughter. It was time to embrace my career ambitions and become a financial advisor. I was a single mom raising a daughter, and what I wanted to teach her more than anything was to follow her dreams and know that anything is possible.

To become a financial advisor, I designed a detailed plan, defining my advisory business. From an academic perspective, the plan was tip-top. It told a story of how I planned to support women to feel confident and empowered in their financial lives and how I would create a comfortable and safe space for women to be part of the money conversation. I was eager and excited to get started, but none of the investment firms saw a place for what I wanted to do. I continued to be turned away.

One bank firm did invite me for subsequent interviews. At the very end of our last meeting, there was one person I had to impress to get offered the position. I sat there on the edge of my seat willing him to say yes to offer me a chance at embarking on this journey. After the formal question part was over, the branch manager relaxed so far back in his chair that I was positive he might tip, and I did all that I could to contain my eagerness. After a long pause, he acknowledged that he appreciated my enthusiasm and could tell I was very passionate. And then the words that came next I will never forget.

"But is there *really* a market for this?" he asked.

My jaw dropped. Tears pricked behind my eyelids. I had to choose my next words carefully for fear I might start crying or maybe even yelling, not knowing in that moment if I was more sad or mad.

I couldn't believe the archaic and patriarchal nature of his statement. *Of course*, there was a market for serving women who wanted to build wealth!

Women make up half the world's population. There are many financially independent women who are the sole financial decision-makers of their households, including me as a single parent. My dream career suddenly felt like a silly daydream that had no place in reality. I was devastated, depleted, and disheartened. This man might not have realized the impact of his statement, but his words hit me like a dagger. As you may have guessed—I did not receive a job offer from him.

Looking back now, I'm grateful for not being offered a position by a man that couldn't see a market for specifically serving women. And I'm grateful for all the people who turned me down, unable to see the need for female-focused advice, because it led me to the place that did embrace my vision. And that's where I hit the ground running.

Two elements of my own life worked in my favor: I had seen first-hand the stress that a lack of money can cause women, specifically; and two, even though this man had rejected my ideas, I knew they were sound. Even if it took me a little while to figure that part out. And so I built my financial practice my way, giving women a safe space to thrive. I started hosting in-person events exclusively for women on various financial topics. And I received a lot of flak from my male colleagues around the office for my "no men allowed" approach.

I didn't care though. I had to give women a comfortable place to talk about money where they wouldn't be ignored. This had to be done.

I cold-called all the other companies in my office and all the neighboring buildings to invite their staff to my inaugural women-only event. On the afternoon of the meeting, I was so nervous that nobody would show up. If I was wrong, and women indeed had no interest, then I would be left with an empty boardroom and a lot of sandwiches and salad. Waiting in that room, the clock nearing noon, I readied the excuses in my head to make myself look like less of a failure to my colleagues when it flopped.

But, as the minutes approached the start time, women flooded out of the elevators onto the 41st floor of my building. I could see them through the boardroom doors, approaching the front desk, saying they were here for the investing session.

Giddy inside, I wanted to jump up and down and shout, *I did it!* But I did my best to keep a cool professional exterior.

Presenting in front of that room full of women was like an out-of-body experience. I was so pumped with adrenaline that I don't even remember how I got through the presentation. But I *do* remember women coming up to me when it was over. One said that she was excited to go home and talk to her boyfriend about the stock markets, feeling more confident than ever. Another woman thanked me for presenting complex concepts in a way that was easy to digest.

They were excited. Not intimidated. This is how I'd hoped women would feel. It was happening. Women were growing confident about their money.

Fast-forward to now, years into building my female-focused business, and I can say I absolutely love what I do. It feels amazing to walk beside my clients as they transform their relationships with money. A thrill washes over me to see the effects of money confidence take hold as women go after their most ambitious financial goals—including funding their first home, defeating their debt, procuring peace of mind with a sizable savings account, establishing an education fund for their children, and going on fabulous adventures around the world. It's all proof that this money and investing stuff actually does work. You can have big bold dreams, and you can achieve them.

The first step is simple: it begins with an unwavering *belief in yourself.* Start with confidence. If money has shown up as a source of stress, shame, disappointment, or confusion in your life up until this point, it might be hard to believe that another way is possible. But it is. You can take control of your money. It's possible to make money your thing.

I share my own story and those of other real women in this book as proof. When you embrace the concepts in the pages to follow and put them into action in your own life, your money confidence will fall into place.

To get you there, this book has been divided into four parts. Part 1, "The Inner Work," calls on you to dig deep in terms of your habits, thoughts, and preconceptions about money. Like so many of us, you're likely carrying some money baggage that has accumulated over the years—you're going to learn how to ditch it. After working through what's been weighing you down, you'll be able to let go of the past. Finally, you'll explore some of the forces that may be keeping you stuck or believing that money success is out of reach. When you can move past money mistakes and let go of comparisons you'll be ready to start your journey.

Part 2 will build your money muscles. And just like you wouldn't start with the heaviest weight when fitness training, you'll work your way up to your money confidence. This section begins by asking you to be open to learning as the first step. Have compassion and be patient with yourself. We often forget that practice is essential to developing a new skill. Just like learning to drive a car can feel completely unnatural at first, the same is true for learning about money and investing. It may feel unfamiliar initially but gets easier with time.

You'll develop an awareness of where you currently are with your money because knowing yourself and where you stand is part of the foundation of money confidence. You can't start *any* journey without first knowing your starting point. It all begins by taking an inventory of what you have, then coupling that with what you're earning and spending. Once you have the awareness, it's time to be open to the power of investing. Confidence grows as your money does, and investing is an integral part of building wealth. If fear has been holding you back from investing, it's time to kick it to the curb. You deserve to reap the rewards of investing and to enjoy watching your money grow.

Once you have established a foundation for your financial confidence through the awareness tools and investing knowledge in these chapters, Part 3 is all about "Making Your Money Confidence Unshakeable." Now that you're on the journey to making money your thing, an important part of keeping you on that path is staying engaged with your money. It's *your* money, and the person who will love and care about it the most will always be you. This means you must pay attention. You need to be a part of the discussions and decisions being made about *your* money. Don't give up control entirely or outsource this important responsibility to someone else.

When you take the lead and become more involved with your money, you won't be thrown off course if you lose your job, are hit with an unplanned expense, or find your investments are impacted by a recession. Acceptance of what you cannot control is key when it comes to your money. Stay focused on what you *can* do in both the short and long term. Make money a priority. Spend time concentrating on financial matters. Spending time with your money builds a strong bond, with no room for fear and insecurities to creep in. Developing a deep understanding of your money is the way to build lasting confidence about your finances. And what better way to spend time with your money than going on a money date?

Having unshakeable money confidence is best experienced from a position of power. Allow yourself to unapologetically step into the role of money boss. As the leader of your finances, you can own your role as a serious earner and smart investor.

By the time you get to Part 4, you'll be excited to talk about your money, embracing it as your thing. And now that you've stepped out of fear and can rise above living in financial survival mode, you might find out that it's about much more than just money. When you look at what you truly want from your money, what emerges are your underlying values. It becomes more than the physical dollar bills or the number reported in your bank account.

Much *much* more. What lies below the surface of your biggest money dreams are the values that you hold dear, such as freedom or adventure.

Congratulations on taking the first step toward making money your thing. Now settle into your favorite chair and put your phone on silent. You're about to embark on a money journey that might change your whole outlook on life.

PART 1

THE INNER WORK

CHAPTER 1

THE EARLY MONEY MESSAGES

IN MY VEHICLE, the rule is that the driver gets to pick what we listen to. So, for trips with me, this usually means an audiobook. My six-year-old daughter is very vocal about her dislike of my audiobooks. On our car rides, I generally opt for a personal growth pick, convinced that she's absorbing important life concepts well ahead of her years. On one particular drive, while listening to *Braving the Wilderness* by Brené Brown, my daughter caught a line that perplexed her.

"Why did she just say we have to hold hands with strangers, Mom?" Ivy asked.

This made me laugh because I tell her to stay away from strangers, and the reality of the global COVID-19 pandemic that surrounded us when we took that drive meant I'd taught her not to touch anything, much less a stranger's hand.

Clearly, this statement went against the messages my daughter had been receiving, and now she was confused. I love that she spoke up. It gave me the opportunity to explain that Brené didn't mean it that way. I imagine she meant to symbolize how we create community and a sense of belonging by connecting with others. My daughter's question gave me the chance to straighten this out with her. To better explain the context but to still make sure she maintained caution.

This conversation got my financial advisor-self thinking. If children are sponges, giving meaning to everything around them, then, of course, money is no exception. Early messages about money can have a big impact. And because of this I began developing strategies to talk to kids about money. Think back to the early messages about money in your household: What do you remember hearing? Were the messages positive or negative? Many of us, myself included, were exposed to negative household conversations about money, which centered on never having "enough," or money being a cause of stress.

As a child, when I took a chance and asked for something, I knew that the answer from my mom would be one of the following:

"That's too expensive."

"We have no money."

Or . . .

"I can't afford that."

Money never was talked about in a positive context in my household back then.

Leading up to my parent's divorce, they had many arguments centered on money. My mom was upset with my dad for not making any effort to get another job after being laid off while she worked four jobs to keep the lights on and a roof over our heads. But the frustration about money in my household didn't subside after my dad left; it just transformed into an inner conflict for my mom to bear on her own.

We were in a constant state of trying to stay financially afloat. And trying to stay afloat summed up the theme for the money conversations that circulated in my home. The primary messages about money that I heard included that we never have enough, that we can't afford to buy nice things, and that money doesn't grow on trees. On repeat.

Do any of these phrases resonate with money messages from your childhood? Or were your early money memories much different, and if so, in what ways? Take a moment to reflect on the following:

In your childhood, what messages about money do you recall hearing?

Did these messages tend to have a more positive or negative theme surrounding money?

The messages themselves may have been harmless. They are only words, after all. But what is more dangerous than the words themselves is what they can morph into.

When young minds try to make sense of words by giving them meaning, like my daughter did when she thought she was being instructed by Brené Brown to hold a stranger's hand, it leaves room for misinterpretation.

As you interpret the words you're hearing and give them meaning, you allow them to come to life. And depending on the meaning you give those words, they might go on to be the hero or the villain in your story. It's their meaning that can wreak havoc in your life, not the words themselves. How you interpret what you hear has the power to inform your beliefs. If all you hear is negative messaging around the subject of money, you may develop the belief that money is bad. Conversely, if you primarily hear positive messaging about money, you may find yourself feeling optimistic about money.

Six-year-old me can attest to the pain which can be caused by negative money messages being misinterpreted. For Christmas that year, I desperately wanted Barbie's dream house. It was the only item on my wish list that year because it was *ALL* I wanted. Commercials for it replayed during the breaks of my favorite cartoons on television. I visualized my Barbies living in that mansion and knew exactly how I would arrange each room.

There would be no need for other toys for Christmas if I got this one wish. I asked Santa for the dream house because it was a big item and my mom had already said it was "too expensive." I had to put my faith in Santa for this one. I was on my best behavior leading up to Christmas, knowing that he would have a close eye on me.

When the special day finally arrived, I awoke early and didn't take my eyes off the clock, willing it to say 7:00 a.m., the time my mom permitted us to go downstairs to open presents. I rushed to the tree to see what new presents had been left by Santa.

I was worried. The new presents looked too small to be the dream house. But I didn't lose hope just yet. I tore into the wrapping paper, certain it would be there. I had done everything right to earn that beautiful pink mansion. My optimism slowly dwindled with each gift I unwrapped, until I opened the last one, only to reveal a pair of blue suede shoes that I was never going to wear.

There was no dream house under my tree.

Heartbroken, I held back my tears. I didn't want my mom to see my disappointment, knowing that it was a present she couldn't afford to buy me.

The next day, I was excited to put the events of Christmas behind me and get out and play with my friend Sammy, who lived in our townhouse complex. I could tell she was eager to see me too as she ran toward me from the snowy playground at the center of our buildings.

"Santa got me the Barbie dream house!" were the first words out of her mouth.

My stomach dropped as I stood in shock. My vision went blurry from tears that were welling up.

I couldn't understand why Santa had given one to her but not to me too. Surely, he had more than one dream house in his workshop.

Prior to hearing about Sammy's good fortune, I had decided that maybe he didn't give out presents that were that expensive. But, clearly, I was wrong. My mind scrambled for an explanation. Why didn't I get a dream house too? What did Sammy have that I did not?

None of it made sense to me and it wasn't fair. I knew I'd done everything right and I still didn't get the dream house.

But Sammy did.

Clearly, I was lacking something. Just like the lack I'd heard about over and over again in my household. Not having enough seemed to blanket my entire existence. And in that moment having less than others took on a much deeper meaning about *me*. I now saw it as a characteristic or quality that described *me*.

"Not enough" enveloped everything around me. It *was* me.

I was part of a family that never had enough, and as a member that must also make me "not enough."

Prior to Christmas that year, Sammy had been my best friend. We loved all the same things. But now, for the first time, I felt a distance between us. We were not the same at all. We were very different. She was one of the special ones and I was not. I was not as worthy as other little girls like Sammy.

And having less meant that I would never be as special. I got ugly shoes for Christmas, while the special girls like Sammy got exactly what was on their wish lists.

I can't deny that this story brings up emotion for me even as I write about it today. I hurt for the younger me, who took on a belief in that moment that she was not enough, that she was worth less than other girls. My heart hurts for all children who grow up in poverty because I know firsthand how easy it is to allow your family's net worth to define your self-worth.

Still, I was only a child, and no child should have to experience doubt about their worthiness. But in that moment, I internalized "not enough" as a description of myself. And it was the false belief from the meaning I attached to the words that did the damage. I took the words in and accepted them as a part of me. They told a story about my worthiness and how I could be categorized in comparison with others.

And although my story centers on what can happen when a young mind tries to make sense of the words used about money when the overarching theme of the words is negative, please keep in mind the words and phrases don't have to be explicitly negative in order to impact your beliefs about money. I've also seen instances of positive money lessons being capable of working against us.

This was the case for Cynthia, a client that came to me in her early fifties, after losing her job due to corporate restructuring. Cynthia hadn't been on the job hunt for decades and she feared that it would be challenging to find work again. I suggested she go through the financial planning process before she allowed herself to get too stressed over the *what-if* scenarios. And turns out, what her financial plan showed was fantastic news. Based on her net worth and retirement goals, she actually didn't need to find another job; she could retire right then. Cynthia was thrilled because, truthfully, she had no desire to go back to work. And getting to see her financial dreams come true meant I was thrilled too!

I wanted to know more about Cynthia's background because I love to share the key successes from real-life financial stories. She said that from an early age, her parents taught her that money was to be saved. And she carried that diligent habit into her adult years and had been aggressively saving ever since her very first job. A seemingly positive money message that she picked up at such an early age, granted her this wonderful gift of financial freedom.

But what followed was where the problem lies.

When I talked to her about setting her investment accounts up to start paying her a monthly cash flow (essentially her retirement paycheck), she kept asking to hold off, that she didn't need it yet. After this continued for over a year, I scheduled a meeting to find out what was up—how she was managing to live on *NO* income.

"Why aren't you using any of your money?" I asked.

"I shouldn't be spending it. I need to be saving it," she replied.

"You were saving for retirement, and now you are retired. So now you get to *spend* it!" I encouraged.

She had a look of concern on her face, obviously not sold on my eagerness for her to spend money. Referencing the tables, we revisited the amounts she could draw down without outliving her resources. Still, she seemed hesitant, even after going through the numbers line by line. I asked some more questions. What became apparent was that she was not giving herself permission to spend money. She had learned very early on that money was *only* to be saved and she had mastered that very diligent habit for decades.

But she hadn't received any guidance on the opposite side of that equation—about how she could spend her hard-earned savings. And so, the positive message about saving money that she learned as a child backfired, in a sense. She was stuck.

Cynthia had a deeply ingrained belief that money should only be saved, and now she couldn't reconcile how she would ever actually spend it. To move forward, she was going to have to unlearn a belief that she had lived by for most of her life.

It's not ideal to have to change a belief as an adult, with years of unlearning to do.

Cynthia and I decided on a very gradual process to get her there, starting with sending her a small amount of spending cash each month, with the goal to slowly increase. It took her some time to get the hang of it, but she's now enjoying the retirement income that's paid to her by her savings.

Mine and Cynthia's stories exemplify the power of early money messages. Even though I'm sure you can identify the flaw in my six-year-old thinking with the Barbie dream house. There's a sharp distinction between my family not having enough and me not *being* enough. And in Cynthia's case—yes saving money is important, *but* you also need to allow yourself to spend it when the time comes.

It might be easy to make these distinctions from an outsider's perspective. But if you heard the messages very early on and took them quite literally, they become your truth.

Reflecting back now, my Barbie dream house story seems trivial. Knowing that there was no man from the North Pole who judged my worthiness based on my family's socioeconomic status. But knowing this now doesn't mean I didn't carry this belief about myself for a long time. The feeling of not enough stayed with me throughout my childhood, lurking below the surface, triggered by certain events. Expensive occasions could cause the unworthiness to flood over me, reminding me I could never fully escape it. The worst times of the year—back to school and holidays. Back to school came with an expectation that you would start the year with all new cool clothes and supplies—a standard I couldn't achieve. And what followed holidays and birthdays was the dreaded question.

"What did you get?!"

Knowing my answer wouldn't impress my interrogators. And scared it would reveal the truth about me—that I had less, that I *was* less. It followed me into my early adult years too. Never being able to fully escape this feeling of not being enough. But, at that point, it became easier to hide. Working full-time allowed me to buy the things that other people had, so it was no longer as easily identifiable. I provided limited details about my upbringing, including the neighborhood I grew up in, and made sure to buy all the brand name items. People were none the wiser. I was just like one of them.

On my journey to become a financial advisor, I had to repair the deep wound of unworthiness that festered from growing up poor. To do this, I had to look within myself.

As my financial advisory practice was blossoming, my income wasn't growing with the business. It was as if I had hit a wall in my earnings potential. Frustrated, I realized I needed to take action. My entrepreneurial spirit was wounded to be working more but making less. I figured that this had to be a signal that the problem was below the surface. That it was time to unpack the money baggage I had been storing away since childhood. A phenomenon I was learning about from the personal growth and development books I was devouring. I decided to do a journaling exercise (which I now encourage my clients to do as well). In the exercise, I recalled some of my earliest money memories to help me understand their origins and how they had gone on to inform my current beliefs about money.

The experience was enlightening and healing. It helped me identify the power of words when it comes to money. I laughed and cried as I remembered being the keeper of my family's grocery budget, saving up to buy a Super Nintendo and asking Santa for the Barbie dream house. It was the first time I was truly able to see the meaning that my young mind had attached to the messages I'd heard about money. Seeing the power I gave to those words, internalizing them as if they were pieces of me.

I'd allowed those messages to become weapons, and the more I believed in them the more damage they caused. Seeing this all come to life on the pages of my journal brought me the greatest gift—awareness. And once I had awareness, I knew what needed to be done.

First, it was time to get rid of the beliefs I took on about money from my childhood. They had to go. Not only because they were completely inaccurate, but because holding on was holding me back.

This exercise, and the gift of awareness it brought, gave me back the power to choose what beliefs about money could stay and what needed to go. I encourage you too to dig deeper into the messages you received about money throughout your childhood—whether they were positive or negative.

Writing about my experiences helped me identify the root of a belief I held about money and worthiness for a very long time. I hope writing about your early memories surrounding money will have a similar healing effect for you. Take the time to investigate the messages that you received about money growing up and the meaning you attached to them.

Did any of those messages have the power to influence your overall thoughts and beliefs about money? And are any of these beliefs still present in your current relationship with money?

What you may discover is that the current beliefs you hold about money aren't even accurate and maybe they aren't even yours (if they came from the messages you heard from family or friends). The beliefs you hold about money may have originated from your young mind trying to make sense of it all. And if that's the case, now is the time to let them go. Take your power back. You get to decide what you want to feel and believe about money. I choose to start feeling worthy and deserving of money, and I hope you do too.

TAKING ACTION

Below are some questions where I encourage you to journal your answers. I'm a strong believer in the power of writing things down over mentally answering in your head. When you write it down you allow for more freedom and space to go deeper into your exploration. And it stays stored on the page as an archive that you can revisit at any time.

Give yourself time and find a quiet space to write out your answers to the following questions. These prompts are designed to help guide you in this exploration, but if you're inspired to add more or change them to better suit your own experience, I welcome you to do so.

- What is your earliest memory of money? Why does this memory stand out to you?
- What kind of relationship did your parent(s) or guardians have with money?
- Growing up, how was money talked about in your household? Were the conversations mostly positive or negative? Was there ever conflict present when it was discussed?
- Did you or someone you love ever have painful or shameful experience surrounding money?

- What were some of the common words that were used when talking about money throughout your childhood? What money messages can you remember hearing?
- What money lessons or advice did you receive from parents or other important influences in your life growing up?
- As a child when you received money as a gift, or earned it as allowance, etc., what did you do with it?

What may emerge for you in this exercise is an awareness of your beliefs around money and maybe even the exact instances of where they originated. It's amazing how influential our young minds can be; even a seemingly minor event can have a significant influence on us. How we can allow words to take on meaning, which can shape our internal belief systems. And what is even more powerful about this discovery process is that you then have the ability to let go of the beliefs that aren't based in reality and that aren't serving you.

Now it's time to take back your power; it's time for you to choose what you want to believe about money. What are the money messages that will support you in living the financial life of your dreams?

After answering the questions above, summarize the beliefs about money that you're letting go of. And now for the best part. It's time to build your own belief system about money, no outside influences necessary. You get to choose. Maybe it's about how you're worthy of receiving prosperity and abundance in all your endeavors, or how you're allowing yourself to save and spend money in alignment with your biggest goals, or how money loves you and that there's no ceiling to your earnings potential, or that there's an abundance of money available to everyone. Spend time writing down the beliefs that you consciously choose to have about money and that will serve you on this journey of building your money confidence:

I am choosing to let go of . . .

I am choosing to believe the following about money . . .

CHAPTER 2

WHERE WILL YOU GO FROM HERE?

YOU'VE HAD A RELATIONSHIP with money that probably started sometime in your youth when you received your first allowance or opened your first bank account. And each money experience—the good and the bad—has brought you here. It's valuable to explore the past and how it's influenced where you stand today in your financial life. But know that the past is just that—*the past*, and it doesn't dictate your journey going forward.

Growing up in poverty and watching my mom's constant battle with money was a crappy start. That may have been where my money journey began, but it wasn't destined to continue that way. You have the power to choose your own destination on your money journey.

I first recognized my right to change course around the age of seven. Monday evenings, my sister and I listened to AM radio play oldies in our outdated Ford Escort while our mom went into the grocery store to get what we needed for the week. I dreaded those trips.

Time dragged on for what seemed like hours. The entire experience could be easily summed up in one word: *boring*.

My sister sat in her designated post in the front passenger seat because Mom said we bugged each other too much when we were both in the back. From my seat I watched the sliding doors of the grocery store, willing the next person exiting to be my mom. The wait always felt like forever.

On one occasion when I was getting extra antsy, I was tempted to make an escape to go find her. I was concerned she'd forgotten her promise to be quick. My older sister, given the responsibility of being in charge, of course, would never let me out.

I didn't understand the need to leave us in the car back then.

But my mom confirmed my suspicions as to why she left us in the car recently when I questioned her about it. She grew tired of having to say "no" to us all the time. Bringing us into the cereal aisle meant she would have to continuously use phrases like "no, you can't have that," "we can't afford that," or "that's too expensive." Onlookers may judge her when we'd press a bit harder with our pleas, unwilling to take her first "no" for an answer. That was when she had to get a bit louder, when she had to take a firmer tone. She got tired of repeating the reality of our finances and putting it on display for others to hear. It was enough for her to remind us on a daily basis. The last thing she needed was the strangers at the grocery store to know about our "situation." And so we waited in the car.

Despite having to refuse our pleas for the extras, it never got easier for my mom. A deep kindness in her eyes told me that she was an ally, not the enemy. She didn't want to have to be the constant bearer of bad news. And so she didn't always give us an immediate "no." Sometimes she paused. She'd twist her lips to the side, her gaze distant, focusing on nothing in particular. I was hopeful during those pauses. Maybe she was considering, perhaps doing the math to see if there was any way she might be able to make it work. But what usually followed was a new version of *no*. Sometimes, it was in the form of a "maybe next time," and sometimes, there was a counteroffer to distract us such as letting us eat dinner in front of the TV that night, but it never really came close to satisfying the want.

Mom stuck to the basics. We didn't get name brands or any extras. Our grocery bill had a strict budget with no wiggle room. The total couldn't exceed what was in our bank account.

One day, when I was allowed to go inside the supermarket, she unblinkingly watched the numbers add up as the cashier rang through our items. Eyes fixed on the register display, Mom requested the subtotal midway through the check-out process. On that grocery trip, the grapes weighed more than expected. They didn't come home with us.

I was mad at those grapes, not knowing where else to direct my disappointment at that moment. To this day, when my daughter asks for grapes on our shopping trips, I'm always curious to see the price they ring in at, never forgetting the financial turmoil those tiny pieces of fruit could cause.

My father left when I was five, before the days of having to wait in the car at the supermarket. He didn't pay child support or contribute any money to raising me and my sister. And without the resources to take this matter in front of a judge, there was little my mom could do to change the situation.

She focused on what she *could* do, which was working hard to provide for us. She had us in her early twenties in the 1980s, when young women often prioritized planning for families after high school. With no postsecondary education, her job prospects were limited. The jobs she held in the early years after she and my dad separated paid her minimum wage.

She was passionate about caring for children, so she got a job in a daycare center. But her income was barely enough to cover our rent, utilities, and food. She also had to pay for before and after-school care for us since we couldn't stay home alone while she worked looking after other people's children. It was like an impossible math calculation each month, with more money going out than coming in. But somehow, she managed to keep us afloat.

Soon, she decided it made more sense for her to run a daycare out of our subsidized duplex. I was thrilled because I wasn't a fan of our babysitter. No more having to force down her soggy pancakes! And it meant I got to see more of my mom. With two kids of her own, by law, my mom was able to watch four other children. This brought in slightly more money than she'd been making working in the daycare center. But the math still wasn't on her side. She was making very little.

When a bill came in the mail, or when she approached a cashier, she fell into her deep concentration mode. I knew not to disrupt her when she was deep in thought. It put her on edge and she was easily annoyed because her mind was occupied by calculations. She reconciled the numbers on a scrap piece of paper she kept on our kitchen counter. It was important that she knew how much money we had, to the penny. Because not knowing could mean overspending. It could mean there wasn't enough left in the account to cover an upcoming bill. There was no cushion. We had zero savings and no credit card. All she had was a small overdraft limit on her account. In those days before online banking, we made many trips to the bank to confirm where the finances stood each month.

I hated going to the bank almost as much as waiting in the car at the grocery store. At the bank, my mom showed me the slip of paper that the machine printed out and explained this reported exactly how much money we had. She didn't hide the account balance from me. And maybe that was oversharing, but it served an important purpose —proof she wasn't lying. When she repeatedly told my sister and me "we have no money," she meant it. I didn't have much context on how much things cost but our number never went beyond the hundreds. I knew this meant we didn't have much money.

Sometimes, while I waited, I would rummage through the garbage bin beside the bank machine and read the crumpled, discarded slips. I wanted to find one with a number lower than ours. It was a money challenge, and I didn't want to be in last place. But I could never seem to find one. I wished we could swap lives with one of the owners of the accounts that had the big numbers, longing to know how they got to be so lucky.

Sometimes, our balance had a dash in front of the total. This, Mom said, meant our account was in overdraft. We had less than no money, and now we actually owed the bank money. She explained that to get back to having money, first we had to pay back the bank what we owed. And only after that would we have money to spend again.

My stomach ached when we were in overdraft. My mind anxiously ran through scenarios of what we might do if we needed money because that meant there would be absolutely *no* spending until payday. Daily, I'd check in with my mom to find out if we managed to escape overdraft. Being back in positive territory brought at least some sense of relief. I cannot even imagine how scared my mom must have been, with how much time we spent in overdraft.

Mom wanted nothing more than to be able to provide for us. I witnessed firsthand how hard she worked and it shaped me. Her diligent work ethic was worthy of an award. Calling in sick was never an option. She pressed on no matter what, on a mission to support her family. But her deep focus on earning enough to keep the house running took her away from us. Even in moments that she was *there* physically with us, I felt the pull of her attention was elsewhere. How could she be expected to be fully present when she was thinking about how to put food on the table? What to do if there wasn't enough to keep the lights on? Or if she couldn't pay the rent?

The weight of financial stress takes a toll on a family and it's a heavy load to carry. I wanted nothing more than to take some of it from my mom so that she could feel confident we'd make it through the month. Seven-year-old me, with a stomach in knots over the helplessness I felt in this financial battle, wanted to relieve some of the burden. No person or family deserves to go through this. And at that time it was especially true for my mom.

I hated the reality of our financial situation. I didn't like waiting in the car at the supermarket. It was embarrassing to put back the grapes, and I was mad at money for stealing my mom's attention away from us. Out of these experiences grew a deep desire to make a change. I had had enough and was ready to do things differently. So I decided to go from being a passive observer to an active participant. And it all started with math.

Being privy to the details of my mom's finances drew me into a fascination with numbers. I wanted to master them because I believed understanding numbers held the key to solving our money problems. I conquered my math lessons easily and swiftly. But grade one math could only take me so far; I needed a bigger challenge. So I begged my sister to share her math problems with me since she was three grades ahead. I loved being able to pull out the important pieces of information to analyze and come up with the solution. I learned long addition, subtraction, and multiplication well ahead of my classmates. I could navigate complex problems like those that told a story of a person making multiple stops on their way to work and having to solve for the time they arrived. In fact, I enjoyed the challenge of it. I was able to figure it out completely on my own. I loved math. It made sense. There was only one answer and I knew if I worked at it, I could figure it out.

One day, when I was feeling particularly confident with the progress of my math skills, I had a brilliant idea. I suggested I use my mental math to help my mom out on the grocery store trips. I told her I'd add up all the groceries tally for her, so she wouldn't have to worry about removing items at the check-out if she spent too much. She paused to consider. A deep line appeared between her eyebrows, which I knew meant she was giving this serious thought. Her gaze was distant as she played out this scenario in her mind.

After a long pause, she said, "Okay, deal."

And with that, I officially became her grocery store helper. It was our ticket in. No more waiting in the car for my sister and me.

My mom provided our shopping budget and it was my job to keep the tally in my head of where we were at with the groceries in our cart. I took the role very seriously. This was one of my most important math assignments yet because being right made a difference. It meant saving the shame of putting back the grapes. I loved knowing that there were ways I could do my part to reduce some of my mom's stress. On my best helper day ever, I came within a dollar.

Mom gave me an impressed eyebrow raise and smiled for a job well done. And that was enough for me.

It felt amazing to contribute. I was no longer only the recipient of the cards I had been dealt; now I was an active participant. I didn't have to simply accept what was, but rather I could step up and help. Instead of following a path of limited options that had been laid out before me, I recognized I had the power to do things my own way.

Poverty was where it started for me. *But* that was only the beginning. A beginning that served a valuable role in finding my passion and purpose. It led me to the work I do today. But I was only able to get to this work by making the conscious choice to change my money journey. Instead of taking the path that was paved by my beginnings, I took a different direction. I chose a new path.

Maybe money showed up as a source of stress and shame in your earliest experiences. Or maybe there was lots of it to go around and you never had to think about it. No matter where and how it all started for you, it doesn't define you. That's merely the beginning of your journey.

You get to decide where it goes from here.

It's time to embrace your power to choose your direction and destination. Because it's *your* money journey. And on this journey, you are permitted to:

- Do things your own way
- Say no
- Make mistakes
- Learn and grow
- Change habits
- Dream big
- And trust in yourself

You are the designer and creator of your financial journey. Nobody but you get to decide how it all plays out. It hasn't been mapped out *for* you.

I'm living proof that poverty is not a life sentence or a cycle that must simply be perpetuated. I changed my journey and picked a new destination. This chapter shared the story of where it all began for me, but *my* turning point was the recognition that I could do it *my* way. And you can too because *your* past doesn't define your future either.

Now my question for you is this: Are you ready to take control of your own money journey and choose your destination?

If the answer isn't a *heck yes*, that's perfect because I wrote this book to get you there, so you're in the right place. Now, where will you go from here?

TAKING ACTION

Your money story has not been set—you get to choose the destination!

Take some time to write about your money journey:

Where does it go from here?

And how do you want to feel about your money at the end of this book/journey?

CHAPTER 3

AND DON'T FORGET ABOUT THE POSSIBILITIES

I**T'S HEARTBREAKING THAT MONEY** has the ability to carry such a negative undertone in so many lives. When people reach out to me for financial advice, they often cite a problem that they are seeking help with as the catalyst. Some common examples of their pain points include a late start on saving, embarrassment that they don't understand money, concern they will never be able to retire, a major life-changing event impacting their original plans, paralysis from overwhelm and confusion, and shame about past money decisions.

If money is at the center of your problems, you may view it as something that's broken and has to be fixed. Or money may be a source of blame—showing up as a destructive force so powerful that it has the ability to negatively impact other elements of your life.

What if you could change all this? What if instead of being consumed by the negativity, all you saw were the possibilities when it came to your money?

If money has shown up in a negative or stressful sense, then you may be skeptical about this transition. This reaction is completely understandable, and I'm prepared to do some convincing to get you there on another path. The best way I know how to do this is to take you back. Way, way back, to when you were a kid.

If you have trouble coming from a place of possibility and hope when it comes to your money—I want you to try to remember what it's like to be a kid again. A lot happens in your life from the time you are a child to your adult years. As you grow up, the financial responsibilities pile on and it becomes very easy to lose sight of the possibilities.

But what if you could go back and rediscover the possibilities? What if you relived your early money wins? Through these early memories, perhaps you can break through the conditioning and get back to that place, the place of endless possibility. A place where you can shed the negativity and instead see money for all it can do. To see money working for you, rather than against you.

Although money first showed up as a source of stress in my home as a child, what soon followed were my early money *victories,* which taught me that money can also be a source of pride and happiness.

For me, uncovering the possibilities began with spending more time at friends' homes. During these childhood playdates, I started to discover I was missing out on more than just grapes. Other families had amazing toys.

And I wanted them too.

At nine years old I was overtaken with envy for my best friend Danielle's gaming system. I, too, wanted a Super Nintendo. Correction, I *had* to have a Super Nintendo. I begged and begged my mom for it on a daily basis. She said "no" five hundred different ways. Getting tired of my persistence, one day she provided a different answer.

"If you want it so badly then buy it yourself," Mom said.

My mind was blown.

I needed a moment of pause to process this. All I could think about was how she hadn't said no.

Did that mean I could get a Super Nintendo?

This possibility shook my entire perception of reality. I *could* have a Super Nintendo, the answer wasn't no!

It was like a massive brick wall between me and the gaming console had been bulldozed to the ground and I could see everything beyond it that was once blocked from my view. There was openness, there was light, and there was *possibility*.

Up until that point I'd grown to expect the negatives. It didn't stop me from trying, but I did already know the answer before the words could escape my mom's mouth. And for the most part, I'd accepted this reality. But not anymore. There was another way and it was up to me. This revelation was thrilling. *And* it meant I could stop insistently asking my mom for things. This was a win-win situation.

First was pricing the Super Nintendo by looking through the flyers on the kitchen table that Mom used for weekly sales and coupons. I cut out a picture of the one I wanted which also came with the game Super Mario World. The ad said it was $155.

This was a lot of money because it was much more than what I was used to seeing on our bank machine receipts. I saved the photo in a tin jar that had some loose change amounting to less than five dollars—leftover from buying candy. But there would be no more wasteful purchases. I now had a very important savings goal.

Having my very own Super Nintendo meant I wouldn't have to wait to visit Danielle's house to conquer Chocolate Island and head to the Valley of Bowser. I would be able to play whenever I wanted.

It was time to make some money. At age nine, my options were limited. I requested money instead of gifts for my birthday and Christmas. I also begged my sister to let me help at her babysitting gigs. I offered to be her babysitting partner in return for 30% of her earnings. She very kindly agreed. Emphasis on her *kindness,* because I usually fell asleep before the parents returned, so I wasn't exactly pulling my weight in the partnership. But I knew my sister had a soft spot for Mario Kart, and she too was excited at the prospect of us having our very own gaming system.

Once I got serious about earning and saving, I found a hiding spot for the tin jar in my closet (we didn't live in the safest neighborhood). Door closed, I would count my money in secret, tracking progress toward my goal. After several months of diligent saving and not spending *any* of it, I had done it. I had enough money to make my major purchase. I couldn't stop smiling; it felt so good. I barely slept that night knowing the Super Nintendo would soon be mine.

The next morning, Mom took me to Future Shop. When we walked through the entrance, my excitement couldn't be contained as I spotted the gaming section at the back of the store. I was off like a shot.

I wobbled under the weight of the large box in my arms. My mom had caught up by this time and asked if I needed help carrying it. I turned down her offer. It was all mine and I wasn't going to let it go.

She asked if there was anything else I wanted to look at. Nope. All I wanted to do was get home as quickly as possible to start playing. The line to pay was short, but even waiting behind two people felt like forever. When it was my turn, my hands shook as I placed the heavy box on the counter. Opening my wallet, I felt rich. I assumed the cashier was very impressed that I was paying with my own money.

She probably had expected I would need my mom to pay for something that expensive.

I'd done it! Walking out of the store, I held my head high with this accomplishment. I had been able to make my own money and buy what I wanted without taking anything away from our grocery and living budget. My sister said I would never have enough. But we were both going to be up late that night, me getting first dibs on Mario meant she would have to settle for his brother Luigi.

This was a turning point in my relationship with money. Up until that point, money had always shown up as a source of stress that I had to watch my mom endure. I hated how it challenged our daily life. But when I was able to see the possibilities beyond my circumstances, something changed. Making a major purchase to buy something that I thought would forever be out of reach shifted my perception. I wasn't limited in that moment, and I didn't have to let that be my reality. If I'd discovered a way to get my Super Nintendo, then that meant that I could do the same for anything I wanted.

I no longer saw limitations. I saw endless possibilities.

My belief in the power of possibilities of money started at the age of nine and kept going from there. My next major purchase was a wonderful dog named Nikki. Then came my very own television for my bedroom, followed by a stereo with a karaoke function that I bought, thinking I was destined to be a singer (not the case). And then I bought my own computer because I was fed up with the embarrassment of handing in assignments hammered out on Mom's antique typewriter.

My mother's beat-up Ford Escort was gifted to me when I turned sixteen, which of course motivated me to save up for an upgrade that wasn't covered in rust. That summer, I pulled double shifts at Subway and Dairy Queen to buy a bright teal Dodge Colt. Then I paid for my entire four-year university program without ever taking out a single student loan, again pulling double shifts, this time between Pizza Hut and Ikea.

That very first major purchase with my own hard-earned cash was so much more than a Super Nintendo. It lit a fire in me that has never stopped. It was a catalyst that sparked belief in myself and my abilities. If I could do something that seemed so impossible and out of reach at one point, so beyond my circumstances and what my financial situation could afford, then I could do anything.

There were no limits and I continued to dream big.

And this is why hearing the early money stories of others touches my heart. Because they are so much bigger than the purchase itself. They open the door to the possibilities. They represent the moment we allow ourselves to believe and dream, where anything is possible.

Sitting down to talk to people about their finances, I don't explicitly ask about their earliest money experiences, but they have a way of coming up in our conversations. I've been inspired by so many other early money stories throughout my career.

I have a client Sarah who paid her house off at the age of thirty-nine, one year prior to her ambitious goal of forty. I was so impressed that I had to know more, to understand where it all began. She shared with me that she'd saved up and bought her very own Cabbage Patch doll when *she'd* been nine. The same age as I had been. Being mortgage free before forty is a big goal, but Sarah dreamed big and never lost sight of the possibilities and it all started with that Cabbage Patch doll.

I urge you to cherish those early money memories, when money was exciting. Go back, and remember what it felt like. Dig deep and spend some time in your memory.

Maybe it was the time you opened your very first bank account. Or, a time when you used your very own money to pick out an item of your choosing from the candy store. Whatever it may be, I'm urging you to remember an instance when you embraced the possibilities when it came to your money. Is there at least one example in your money memories when you believed anything was possible and allowed yourself to dream big?

Perhaps you have to go way back, or maybe the memory is more recent for you. How old you were doesn't matter, nor what the end result was. It's about embodying the mindset that anything is possible and nothing is standing in your way.

Everyone has the power to change their perception about money. It doesn't require an early win to be able to see money from a place of possibility. You too have the power to change your relationship with money and make it work for you. From exactly where you are, starting right now. And even if you cannot draw on a specific money win from your childhood there might be a similar willingness to believe in yourself when it came to a youth hobby or sport.

Whether your money journey started at nine, or you're saving for your first big item now, I still invite you to go to that place of possibility that can often be rediscovered from the place of innocence—when you were young. Before you had to take on the adult responsibilities of life. Before you allowed limiting views from those around you to inform your own belief in yourself.

Would you believe that a woman in her mid-twenties could buy a Lamborghini (with her own hard-earned cash)? Guess what, she sure can! And I know this because she's my client. At a lunch meeting with Lyndsay, she caught a glimpse of Benny the Bentley (what I named my dream car), who occupies the background photo on my phone. Yes, most parents reserve this exclusive space for pictures of their little ones, but I'm using it to manifest that sleek, white beast. Anyway, a sly smile spread across her face when she saw Benny, and I knew something good was coming.

"Okay, on the topic of dream cars, can I tell you something?" Lyndsay asked.

"Tell me!" I said, the suspense killing me.

Lyndsay revealed she'd purchased her dream car this past summer—a Lamborghini! She confessed she had no idea that's what her day had in store when it began by going to Walmart to get the best price on pasta noodles. But why not stop at the Lamborghini dealership after saving all that money discount shopping right? I was thrilled for her. As a rock star entrepreneur, I admired her work ethic and drive, and I was so proud of her for making that dream a reality. Lyndsay believed in the possibilities when she stepped into that swanky dealership and I urge you to do the same with your biggest money goals.

This is how your money confidence journey begins. First, you must believe it's possible. If you don't, then nothing else in this book will matter. The journey must start by being open and believing. So I'm asking you to dig deep and approach money with the innocence of a child—when anything and everything was possible. You can, and will, be cruising in your dream car, chilling on the beach, or experiencing whatever that big dream is for you.

TAKING ACTION

Believe in the possibilities, there are no limits on your journey.

Take a moment to write down your biggest money goals.

And if you're open to taking it one step further, I urge you to actually visualize yourself having or experiencing whatever you wrote down (how awesome does that feel?).

CHAPTER 4

TURNING "MONEY MISTAKES" INTO MONEY WISDOM

AS YOU DO THE INNER WORK what may come up are your money demons (aka money mistakes). A big part of why you haven't felt confident about making money your *thing* up until now could be the result of these blasts from in the past. Maybe you bought a car that turned out to be a lemon, purchased your home at the peak of the market, never entered that swanky gym once during your yearlong membership, or took your Vegas shopping trip to another level thanks to those deliciously refreshing slushy drinks.

Whatever it was, you're not alone. We've all had money moments we look back on wishing our Fairy Godmother of Finances had appeared just in time to confiscate the credit card. And perhaps the experience was so bad that it left a lasting impact as it did for Ashley, a woman who hesitantly came to meet with me a few years ago. Her pain point being that she was too scared to do anything, and so her cash sat on the sidelines. When I asked about her goals, Ashley said that she had no upcoming requirements for the money and that it was her long-term savings toward her retirement goal. At the time she was in her early thirties and she wanted to be able to retire in her late fifties.

I was excited to be having the conversation when she still had a twenty-year-plus window for her goal because it meant the power of compounding interest was on her side. This much time was also a gift in terms of the flexibility of the investment options to make her cash grow. Generally in the world of investing, the longer your time frame, the more risk you can potentially take on in your portfolio. Historically, investment returns have shown us that time reduces volatility, so the more time you have the better!

The idea of more risk might spook you—and you're probably wondering why would anyone want to take on risk when it comes to their money. The reason is based on the risk and return relationship of investing, which generally works as follows:

lower risk = lower potential return,
higher risk = higher potential return

With no upcoming requirements for the cash, Ashley had the ability to take on more risk at this point in exchange for higher potential return. Based on those factors, it was clear to me that creating an investing plan for her long-term savings strategy was key to getting her money working toward her goal. Ashley was certainly doing the right thing by putting money away each month but at this rate, she would have to put away far more each month in order to reach her ultimate goal or she would have to push out her target date. Since the entire balance had remained as cash for the past five years, any level of investing would make a difference by adding the power of compounding growth.

To give some perspective on the growth she'd already missed out on, had her cash been invested and grown at a rate of 9%[1] annually over these past five years she could have been about $50,000 richer!

It was time to take action. I didn't want to see Ashley falling short of her goal due to sitting on the sidelines.

I was pumped for Ashley, envisioning all the possibilities available to her. With her timeframe and compounding growth on her side, she could have a fabulous retirement nest egg with the help of some investing. I envisioned her living it up in retirement, lunching with the ladies after a lovely little shopping trip, and heading to the beach to flee the cold winters.

While I cheerfully discussed the benefits of investing to build her wealth, Ashley cowered in her chair, as if she was physically trying to run away from our conversation. Of course, I wanted nothing more than to make her feel comfortable and at ease in our chat about her money. But I could tell she didn't share my enthusiasm and was shutting down. So I paused and asked if she would be willing to share what she was feeling.

Looking down as she fiddled with her purse strap, Ashley explained hesitantly that investing made her nervous based on a past experience that turned out to be "*really, really, really stupid.*"

I empathized and shared that many people come to me with that same fear from something they experienced firsthand or heard about

1   Annual gain in the S&P500 between 1965 and 2021 was 10.5%, https://www.berkshire hathaway.com/letters/2021ltr.pdf

from someone else. It's something I come across far too often unfortunately and so I assured her she was definitely not alone in having reservations.

This seemed to put her somewhat at ease and she elaborated on her really (x 3) "stupid" investment. She explained that several years ago she joined a few colleagues for a Friday lunch at the pub below their office tower. Two of her male colleagues were bragging about how much money they were making on their investment in a mining company stock that was set to strike gold in no time. They bought the stock at $0.10 per share and those shares were now trading at $1 and rising. They kept throwing out projections of what it could go to, one thought it would be at $50/share within the next few months and the other predicted $100/share.

This sounded amazing and piqued Ashley's interest. The company already had proven to do well for her colleagues and they seemed extremely confident that it would keep going up. She had never invested in a stock before but had been wanting to get started investing for some time now and this seemed like the perfect opportunity.

Ashley had been diligently putting away money from each paycheck, a habit her mother had started on at a young age that she carried into her adult years. And so she was sitting on a nice bit of savings accumulated to make her very first investment. She asked her colleagues for the name of the company and then that very next week she opened an online investment account with her bank. She was nervous to enter the trade herself so she called the helpdesk to walk her through buying the stock.

For the first few weeks, she followed the stock price daily, watching it move up and down slightly. Then after about a month of owning it, the price plummeted in a single day to a point where it was trading at next to nothing. Ashely's heart sank when she saw her account balance. This had to be a mistake. She'd never even considered that she could lose her entire investment. Turns out there was no gold to be found, the mine was a dud, the company went bankrupt, and her entire $10,000 investment was wiped out.

Ashley was devastated. She felt nauseous over losing her hard-earned savings. She was ashamed and regretted following the advice of her colleagues without doing any of her own research. The loss left a lasting pain and she knew she never wanted to experience something like that *ever* again. So she decided to avoid investing altogether from that point on, to protect herself from having to relive what she described as "the biggest money mistake" of her life.

My heart hurt, hearing her recount this terrible experience. I wished I had a time machine to do something to protect her from the loss. If there was some way I could have intervened to explain the importance of doing your homework before investing, not putting all your eggs in one basket (more on diversification later), and only allocating what you can afford as well as willing to lose on high-risk bets or gambles.

The stress that it caused her lingered even though years had passed. This one event had the power to shape her entire perception about investing. Instead of seeing it as a means to grow her wealth and help her reach her goals, she saw it as a hurricane wreaking havoc and destruction on its path.

This is a very real danger of letting one misstep shape how you'll behave with your money. Being caught up in a mistake may have you failing to take action or to make forward progress for fear of repeating your error. This was true for Ashley, whose soured stock pick had her giving up on investing altogether.

And avoidance isn't the only byproduct of stewing over a money mistake. Another risk is shame. Too often people keep these moments of their "biggest regrets" or "mistakes" to themselves, locked away in their secret vault. Internalizing and dwelling on mistakes may lead you to develop shame around the topic of money, where one wrong move turns into a label about you. And this is what leads to sweeping statements such as:

"I'm just not good with money," and, of course, the dreaded, "money just isn't my thing."

Giving money blunders this much weight means shame could be limiting your wealth potential. You need to talk about the money demons rather than bottling them inside. Talking about them is the first step to letting them go. Because staying hung up on a past mistake doesn't get you any closer to achieving your goals. In Ashley's case, it meant missing out on the possibility of $50,000 of growth.

Being vulnerable and talking about past mistakes not only helps you, but it can serve to help those around you as well. Sharing experiences with your community helps to normalize, to know that you are not alone. It's a reminder that money bloopers are part of life. And I would also go so far as to say that *everyone* has made some sort of money blunder in their lifetime, myself (who is writing this book about money!) included.

I . . .

Spent my entire summer savings at age seventeen on a sweet stereo, equipped with enough bass to rattle my car, only to have it stolen a few months later (didn't leave any room in the budget for an alarm!); the rap music never sounded as good after that.

Traveled all the way to Europe in my early twenties to visit an English boy I met in Vegas. I was a sucker for the accent (spoiler alert—it wasn't true love).

Got carried away furnishing my first apartment living solo and opted for the "do not pay for twelve months" deal to push it off to the future when I was bound to have more cash (at 20% interest, I paid $2,400 extra).

Avoided the task of creating a budget for far too long.

Moved to the expensive city of Vancouver at the age of twenty-two, which I funded entirely with my credit card and it took me two years to pay it off.

And didn't use all the brilliance I was learning in my finance courses at university to start investing early.

If you've splurged on a luxury that you regret, spent beyond your means, made a poor investment, or were or are late to the game in getting started, you're not alone. We *all* make mistakes.

Perfection is not a prerequisite to financial success. Diligence and consistency can get you there. Mistakes will happen along the way. And that's completely okay and to be expected. But don't let the mistakes become roadblocks that cause you to give up.

Although Ashley was thrown off course by an investment that didn't pan out, all hope was not lost. We were still able to work together to create a plan to get her invested gradually, in a way that was suitable and comfortable for her.

Does knowing that you don't have to be flawless with your money bring you relief?

It should. Give yourself permission to start with a blank slate, free from the weight of shame. Let this be the start of a new relationship with your money based on positivity and possibility.

In this new relationship, there's no room to dwell on miscalculated money moves. Your energy and focus are better directed to what you want more of, not things you would rather forget. What if we find a way for you to move past them by rebranding them?

The words *money mistakes* are in quotations in this chapter title for a reason. Neither you nor I can judge what qualifies as a mistake when it comes to your money. It's subjective. Each of us has different criteria to define a "mistake." And the word itself gives it a negative connotation. When you label something a "mistake" it doesn't exactly give you the warm fuzzies inside. You've been taught that they are bad, not something that you should embrace and be proud of, but something you must actively work to avoid.

Let's not forget they can teach valuable lessons. So turning away from them simply because they have been called a "mistake" would be a loss to the learning opportunity. Instead, you can lean in and embrace the wisdom that each instance offers. A change in perspective is exactly the way to do this.

It's time for a reframe. From this point on, I encourage you to shift your focus off of "money mistakes" and replace it with "money wisdom."

When you're making money your thing there are only money lessons. And the lessons are a gift that leads to money wisdom. From there you expand, and you'll be better off because of this growth.

This might not feel natural. I'm asking you to see the good in a situation that normally may have had you spending days, weeks, or even years beating yourself up over. This is indeed a mindset shift. It will take some getting used to. But what do you have to lose other than feeling like crap?

To help you make the shift, here are some ideas to keep the focus on the positive and possibility, as you build your money wisdom.

Ditch the Guilt

Not saying this will be easy. I suspect the next time you encounter what you previously would have classified as a "money mistake"—you might revert right back to trash-talking yourself. Allowing money guilt to rear its ugly head with the pit in your stomach that radiates with queasiness at the thought of looking at your bank balance, the avoidance tactic of changing the subject or removing yourself from any money conversation, or allowing the inner mean girl to tell you how terrible you are with money over and over and over again. When a money situation doesn't go as planned, your go-to emotions may be regret, shame, blame, anger, or disappointment. These feelings are perfectly normal, as I learned from my fabulous life coach, who encouraged me to *feel all the feelings*—even those that society typically labels as "bad." But you don't want to stay stuck in those feelings. The danger of staying stuck in them is you may start to believe them as more of a personality characteristic, defining who you are. "I made a bad purchase" becomes "I *am* bad with money." I'm sure there are things in your home that scream *waste of money*, but that doesn't mean you are unfit to have a credit card.

Living in guilt will only breed more negativity, and then you become stuck. Let's say you're feeling guilty for not getting an earlier start. You're in your late thirties and other people you know around your age are already well into building their wealth. If you're consumed by guilt you may decide that it's too late, you missed out, and give up hope of ever being able to retire. You let guilt crap on your financial future. But, if instead you make a decision to move through the negative emotions, to let them go, and to move on, you create space for solutions. *Of course*, it's not too late, you can take action to start today! With a clear and open mind, you welcome an abundance of possibilities for your money.

Find the Lesson

Looking for the lesson may be hard at first. But I urge you to try, because that reframe may be the kick in the butt you need. Suppose you would like to work on your spending habits so you can find more to save. Maybe the most recent perpetrator was that pair of designer pumps that numb your feet thirty minutes into wearing them. You recognize they might not have been the most practical use of your resources, and the guilt sets in. Okay, no problem, let's find the lesson. Maybe next time you vow to do a few more trial laps around the store to feel them out or take a day or two to decide if the shoes are a wise addition to your wardrobe. *Ta-da!* Lesson learned. You've grown wiser from the experience and created some essential criteria on what makes the cut. Dig deep for the knowledge nuggets that can be found in all your money experiences because those lessons compound your wealth wisdom.

Spill the Beans to Someone You Trust

People are more than willing to talk about money when things are going well. When someone can turn their home business into the next Apple or Amazon, those are the juicy stories we like to hear. The same isn't true for the messy ones. Hearing about a maxed-out credit card doesn't carry the same thrill as becoming a self-made billionaire. And so many vow to take their money horror story to the grave. But holding it in is a lot of weight to carry. Getting it off your chest by communicating openly provides a sweet relief similar to removing shapewear at the end of your day. Sweatpants never felt so good! This is the entire premise of counseling, psychology, and life coaching—talking through it. Although the default may be to bottle it in thinking nobody wants to hear about your money problems—chatting to someone you trust could be the best way to move past it. The key here is someone you *trust*. Be picky about who you choose to have the vulnerable money talks with. An ideal candidate is empathetic, nonjudgmental, trustworthy, supportive, and maybe even with a good sense of humor—so you can have a laugh about the time you flew to Europe for the British boy only to be ditched (at least you got to see the Eiffel Tower!). And if nobody is coming to mind that exudes the above qualities, try journaling about it instead. In your writing explore the money mishap, how you felt about it, and any advice that you imagine a fabulous bestie might offer so you can work through it, and send it on its way.

Be Grateful

Gratitude is a powerful way to shift out of negativity. This works in all aspects of life including your finances. Instead of being blue—by focusing on the loss, giving up, or feeling like a failure. Can you instead give thanks for the lesson and see the experience from a place of gratitude? Here are some examples:

I am grateful that I learned the power of how compound interest can work against me, that ugly interest charge reminded me to pay off my credit card each month.

I am grateful that I am now aware of the need to save for my future—better late than never.

I am grateful that I was reminded of the importance of protecting my money by being selective about whom I lend money to when my useless ex failed to repay me for his share of the rent.

I am grateful that I now know how important it can be to have savings on hand after having to take a loan to cover a house repair.

I am grateful to have learned that going shopping when I am in a bad mood isn't the best form of therapy; a good laugh with a friend is a much more cost-effective solution.

Try on some gratitude to stop those negative thoughts from spiraling. We truly all do have something to be grateful for, and giving your attention to that feels a heck of a lot better.

Instead of having such negative beliefs around money mistakes, why not embrace your missteps? Share your money bloopers and be proud of the lessons learned and the value those experiences have in your life and the lives of others. It's through these lived and learned experiences that you become a money master.

TAKING ACTION

Say goodbye to the mistakes for good to embrace your money wisdom. Grab a piece of paper and divide the page into three columns. Label the columns as follows: mistakes, learnings/lessons, and gratitude. Then spend some time reflecting on past money boo-boos that stand out in your mind. In the first column, you'll describe the circumstance. Then in the second take time to discover the lesson. And in the third write what you're grateful for about what the experience has taught you or how you grew or changed from it.

Mistakes	Learnings/Lessons	Gratitude

CHAPTER 5

YOU DO YOU

THIS LAST PIECE OF the inner work challenges you to shed societal influences about money and wealth, to make this about *you*. Notice I called the book *Make Money "Your" Thing!* I didn't call it *Make Money Like Other People Do*. Or, *How to Follow the Crowd When It Comes to Your Finances*, or anything along those lines because that wouldn't be about *you*. Making money *"your"* thing is about acknowledging that will be different and unique for each one of you reading this book. And that's the point!

There isn't a standard formula to follow when it comes to your money. Life pressures exist all around you already—from body image, to how to be the best employee, partner, or parent. The outside world, from sources like social media, suggests on a daily basis that you don't measure up or you aren't doing enough.

This book has been written to help you feel uplifted and full of awesomeness about your money. That's why I can't stress enough that it's not about being a money copycat. Comparing your savings or the stuff you buy to your neighbor is a great way to make yourself feel like garbage. Keeping up with the Joneses has quickly become keeping up with the Kardashians—and if you hold yourself to this measure, if you don't achieve billionaire status in your twenties, you're a failure.

Judging your economic success by comparing it to someone else's doesn't work because everyone's goals are so different. I've met with hundreds of people to discuss their finances over the years and I can tell you no two people were ever the same. There's never been a meeting where I felt a sense of déjà vu in what was being shared.

But that doesn't stop people from looking to the crowd to decipher if they are succeeding in the money game. There's no such thing as a wealth benchmark to follow for your finances. So looking around to measure your money mastery will only leave you reaching for the Ben & Jerry's (chocolate chip cookie dough all the way for me).

Being a money copycat will hold you back. Constantly looking to gauge your progress externally will keep you from getting to a place of confidence and empowerment about your finances. I first had this ah-ha moment about five years ago sitting down with a couple, Jill and Jack, who were in their early forties. When I shook their hands, the first thing I noticed was the stack of beaded bracelets on Jack's wrist, which I thought was cool since I too am a big believer in the energy power of wearing crystals.

The couple had a light and breezy vibe about them and I knew they'd be a fun team to work with. Right off the bat, Jack teased about how it was his mother who coerced him to speak with a financial advisor to get *"serious"* about their finances. It reminded me of my own protective mother who still texts me to caution about extreme weather conditions as if I don't have a weather app or can't look out my window. The couple shared details about their careers and their family. Jack said he hoped I'd be able to help them get rich quick because he was ready to retire any day now, to which Jill rolled her eyes.

Jill, the more serious of the two, said she enjoyed her career as a chiropractor but there was a physicality requirement which meant she likely wouldn't be able to continue working much beyond the age of sixty. They also mentioned they had two young children and were keen on being able to cover the costs of their postsecondary education, although Jack joked that he'd only pay if his daughter actually attended school. I appreciated this opportunity to get to know them and experience the lighthearted banter between the two as they shared their goals and priorities with me.

But as much as they were open to sharing, when I got down to asking specifics on the numbers for my projections of their financial goals, they offered up details apologetically. They gave me the numbers but then followed up with a long-winded explanation as if they were concerned they were about to get in big trouble.

Trust me, I'm one of the least intimidating people you could ever meet, so their hesitation was surprising. They struck me as a couple who embraced their uniqueness and followed their own path. But when it came to their money they weren't confident in owning that individuality. Throughout the conversation, they kept searching my face for an indication of how they were doing.

Were they getting it "right"? Were they passing the test?

There was an underlying sense of insecurity and embarrassment as they followed up their answers with statements like:

"But we probably should have more saved by now?" and *"We're behind other people our age, correct?"*

They turned the questions back to me as if trying to seek my approval or validation. And it was in that moment that it all clicked for me. I finally understood this hesitation that I had been coming across for years. Jill and Jack desperately wanted to fit in, to keep up, to do it "right."

They were so hyper-focused on trying to copy others in where they were *supposed* to be with their finances that they weren't even acknowledging their own needs or celebrating their successes.

Allowing peer pressure to dictate your financial achievements is dangerous. Comparing and copying create insecurities about where you stand with your money. It may include guilt over the gap between where you think you *should be* when it comes to your wealth and where you're at. Feeling like you're falling short can put you in a constant state of fear and anxiety about your money. Jealousy and envy can also cloud your own vision and goals when you're laser-focused on what other people have—whether it's the colleague that bought a brand new BMW, the regular house cleaning service all your friends seem to have, or your neighbor who can afford to DoorDash every meal. Keeping the focus on others can have you playing small, not investing, or not saving, creating negative implications on your financial life if that is the case.

There are several dangers to striving to fit in or follow the crowd. Here are few:

Losing sight of what *you* actually want: Perhaps you look at other boss women your age and see that they own a home, have two big family vehicles, and wear only designer labels. Suddenly you find yourself perusing the dealerships to buy the biggest SUV on the lot. But when the first giant monthly payment hits your account, you question why you made this splurge, when your kids fit into your previous ride just fine.

When you're ultra-focused on following the crowd, you might find yourself going after things that aren't important to you. Letting the actions of others direct *your* financial journey will not get you to your goals. You're on your own path; there's nobody you need to follow. A unique money story has brought you to where you are, and you have your own distinct future financial desires. For me, it's saving for Ivy's college so she doesn't have to pull double shifts like her momma did at Pizza Hut and Ikea to pay tuition. Honor your uniqueness, and keep the focus on what *you* want for your money.

Avoidance and procrastination: This can happen when you sense you're nowhere near *where you're supposed to be*. If you feel like the goalposts are too far out of reach, you might have the urge to give up or avoid the topic of finances altogether. Taking a head-in-the-sand approach when it comes to your money. Doing nothing, and maybe even hiding from acknowledging that something needs to be done. If you put off addressing financial matters, you're missing out on letting your money grow over time, as sure as if it were stuffed in your mattress, losing value with inflation by the minute. Allowing the pressure to paralyze you from taking any action has the opposite effect of building wealth. A do-nothing approach when it comes to your money will not get you any closer to achieving your goals and aspirations.

Fear of failure: Mimicking your neighbors when it comes to your money can stir up negative emotions if you sense you're not measuring up. The biggest being fear-based, such as:

> *Fear of doing it wrong*
> *Fear of making a mistake*
> *Fear of being judged*
> *Fear of falling behind*
> *Fear of failure*

When it comes to your financial life, there's no manual, so who's to say if you're doing it *right?*

There's no rulebook that states that before you turn forty you should have X dollars in your retirement savings account. What you can save depends on your individual situation. Personal finance books can offer opinions and recommendations. But those are just suggestions. You still get to take from them what you choose.

There will always be an element of choice, and there's no hard-and-fast right or wrong. Understanding money is personal and different for everyone should help you remember that it's not about winning or losing, or getting it right or wrong—it's about forging your own path to get to where you want to go.

Now that some of the dangers have been highlighted, let's embrace healthy, more productive approaches you can take so you don't feel the need to be a money copycat.

The first step to overcome peer pressure is to acknowledge and accept that it has been impacting your financial life. It's completely okay if getting a glimpse inside the closets of the *Real Housewives* have you feeling down. You may not explicitly know the bank balances of those around you, but it's easy to jump to conclusions about how much money someone has from what they own. And if you fear you may get sick with envy if you see another celebrity carrying a Birkin bag, your feelings are valid and lend themselves to further exploration.

Take time to investigate where the feelings are coming from. Do you remember a time in the past when you first felt these feelings? Maybe it takes you back to your childhood when being accepted by your peers was vital to getting through your school days and saved you from eating lunch solo in the cafeteria. But remember this: you are no longer that kid. Plus eating by yourself eventually feels like well-deserved "you-time" when you have children, a demanding career, or both. And is it really so bad that you don't own a handbag that could cost you as much as a house?

Acknowledge the feelings because they're real. But now that you've traced them way back to when "fitting in" felt essential for survival, you may realize they aren't based in your current reality. Gone are the days of friendship groups and teen drama. You've progressed to that stage of life where you can wear a messy bun and sweatpants to the grocery store and still feel fab (or is that just me?). But my point is the need to follow the crowd might be more of a programmed pattern from your past, rather than a conscious choice. Take a pause and remember it's safe to be you. Your money choices can come from a place of authenticity. Taking action from a place of self-acceptance has a powerful impact on building wealth. But don't be surprised if the "shoulds" or insecurities still creep in—how you *should* be taking more vacations, own more designer clothes, have no debt, or be making a bigger salary at this stage of life. You'll have to resist the instinctual pull to look outside of yourself and avoid the temptation to judge based on what others have or what they're doing with their money. This isn't about them. This is your journey. And it's your money.

Give yourself permission to be you and design your money moves around your individuality. Embrace what's right for you. Are you happy driving an older model car, or do you get pleasure out of having the latest and greatest? Do you dream of traveling the world a few weeks per year, or will you tent at the local lake? Are you willing to put in the work to be the CEO, or do you want to clock out at five and be done for the day?

I have a wonderful client, Paula, who based on her salary assumed she couldn't save as much as others her age. But she refused to let that stop her from taking action. In a review meeting, Paula shared that times were tough when her children were young. Her husband walked out when the kids were four and six, leaving her a single parent.

She received very little child support from him over the years and so she had to step up as the sole financial provider to her son and daughter. She worked at a corporate job downtown but with childcare costs and all the other expenses of life, there wasn't much left at the end of each month. Even still, she recognized the importance of doing what she could to save for her long-term goals, accepting it might be less than what other corporate professionals at her age were saving.

Paula started by putting away $25 per month, all she could spare at that time. She continued adding this $25 each month to her retirement savings account for several years. As her children got a bit older, her costs came down slightly, so she increased what she saved—a little at first—growing her deposit to $50 per month.

But then $50 became $100, then $200, and $300, and so on over the years, to the point where she had amassed enough in her growing retirement investments that she was on track to financial freedom in her late fifties.

Paula could have easily decided to forgo saving in those challenging years, when what she was able to put away each month didn't seem like much compared to her peers. Instead, she did what she could, embracing what was realistic for her. Creating a habit that she stuck with each and every month, despite all the other financial obligations (and she had many).

Do what works for you, even if you're in a place that feels like it's not the best time to start. Building her savings as a single Mom to two young children was not the best time for Paula to start, but she did it anyway. It's not about getting caught up in where you think you should be. Embrace being uniquely you. When you're confident in your individuality you don't hold back or wait to see what the collective does. You do you.

Start now. Exactly as you are because it's your money and you're on your own unique journey. One small action. Do something today to take you one step closer to your financial dreams. Or better yet— I challenge you to do it right now.

That's right. Put this book down!

Right . . .

Now.

Okay, if you took me up on the challenge above, I'm so proud of you, and if I could I would reach out from the pages of this book and give you a big hug! And if you didn't, I'm not letting you completely off the hook; try thinking of one thing you can do and put it on your calendar.

One small step might not seem like a big deal, but I want you to know it is. It was for Paula, who started by putting away the equivalent of five coffees per week, and it can be for you too. Wealth is built by the accumulation of small steps. And it starts with just one.

Acceptance and taking action are two effective strategies against the urge to keep up with the Joneses. But the way to get rid of unfair comparisons and copycatting for good takes a full shift. It involves truly embodying your money uniqueness.

Speaking with people about their finances on a daily basis, I know firsthand how different and unique each person or couple can be when it comes to their financial life. That's one of my favorite parts of the job, that each meeting is so different. New problems to solve, new strategies to develop, and new plans to create. Never a dull moment!

Everyone has their own money history, distinct goals, aspirations, and dreams for their future. Embracing money uniqueness starts by getting rid of all comparisons. Because they don't exist when you realize there's nothing to compare to. You don't have to copy anyone. There are no instructions when it comes to forging your own path. Decide what you truly want. And then allow that to be your guide. Embracing your money uniqueness requires:

Being unapologetically you: You don't owe any explanations when it comes to following your own financial dreams. That's the best part about money uniqueness; it's all about you getting to be you. Maybe you want the luxurious honeymoon in Bora Bora, or maybe you opt for a romantic weekend road trip adventure. Maybe you have your eyes set on the dream sports car typical of a

mid-life crisis, or maybe you save yourself from the instant depre-
ciation by sticking to the previously owned lot. Maybe you want
to live in a home that has more bathrooms than people living
in it, or maybe you prefer the trendy compact condo steps away
from your downtown office. Whatever you have your financial
sights set on, embrace it; no need to justify what you want.

Stay focused: It's easy to get distracted along the way with all the
bright and shiny objects around you—the Mercedes Benz, Louis
Vuitton bag, and the luxurious mansions featured on *Selling
Sunset* (not to mention the outfits!). But it's not about overex-
tending yourself or giving in to the biggest fads. If you're going
after all that "stuff" for the wrong reasons, when the thrill wears
off all you're left with is the depressing credit card statement.
Keep the focus on what you truly want; it might be what you see
someone else have, but it also might be something completely
different.

Be okay with being different: There are so many perspectives
and opinions out there when it comes to money, so embracing
your uniqueness may not be an easy endeavor. In fact, it might
be really *hard* to do. Following your own dreams might mean
standing out from the crowd, and that can feel uncomfortable
or awkward. Let's say you decide that you never want to own a
home. You're happy renting because it gives you so much flexibility. But then when you reach the age of thirty-five, you notice
everyone around you seems to own their homes. You opted not
to be a homeowner, but now you start to question if you're off
track or doing something wrong. As people start to ask you when

you're planning on buying a home the pressure starts to build; you make up excuses to divert answering. You don't feel comfortable offering the truth, which is "never." Being ultra-focused on the opinions of others won't get you any closer to achieving your financial goals. And it might take you further from them if you fall into the trap of following the crowd. Be okay with being different!

Embracing your money uniqueness feels good because it's about aligning with what you truly want. But this doesn't necessarily mean your goals will come naturally or be easy to accomplish. If you've allowed the opinions and actions of others sway your money moves up to this point, that's understandable. And it's also okay if you don't yet know what it is that you want. We aren't often encouraged to explore the unique parts of self and to honor our authenticity, and money is no exception. But it's time to change that. Now is the time for you to discover and embrace your unique financial dreams.

Digging deeper into the details of your wealth goals can help you get really specific on uncovering your money uniqueness. I might say I love to shop, and perhaps you love it too, but the details might uncover much more about our individual preferences. I learned the importance of getting curious in a goal-planning conversation with my client Victoria. In that meeting, we talked about how we both love to travel (fun-related travel specifically, not the business kind), which then didn't seem very unique, but wait for it . . .

As she listed off an array of her upcoming destinations I felt inclined to stop her to get a better understanding of her travel itineraries.

I asked, "How many trips do you take each year?"

"I take one trip per month, so at least twelve per year," she responded.

That was a big number, much higher than my own idea of what it meant to *love* travel. Her goal didn't diminish my love for travel. It highlighted that we truly are all very different when it comes to our financial goals—even if on the surface it sounded like we were the same. So, as you open up to the idea of accepting and embracing your own money uniqueness, don't be afraid to dig deep and get really specific on the details. Because it's in the details where you'll truly uncover *exactly* what you want.

I want to share an activity to get you really thinking about your own money uniqueness. But before I get there I want to remind you that embracing your uniqueness is about you going within. The answers don't lie outside of yourself. No more taking the lead from others. Nobody can direct your financial journey. And that includes the experts, professionals, and me too. Yes, even I can't be the boss and dictate your financial future. I support and help people to achieve their goals, but I learned early on in my career that I cannot tell people what they are "supposed" to do.

This lesson came from my very ambitious client, Tara. As an entrepreneur, Tara was creating an empire and building wealth quickly, and she was only in her early twenties. We decided to grab a salad for our check-in meeting since we both managed to work right through our lunches. I was amped for our chat and could barely hold back the good news as we placed our orders. In the analysis I had done before the meeting, I discovered Tara was well on her way to achieving millionaire status before she turned thirty. I couldn't wait to tell her how she would be free from work in no time!

Around this same time, I had become very intrigued about the FIRE movement. FIRE stands for financial independence, retire early. It's an entire movement dedicated to gaining financial independence and retiring early. And I mean really early—as in the thirties and forties kind of early. As a financial professional, I'm all about seeing people reach their goals, and the earlier the better. One of the keys to this movement is about being diligent with keeping expenses low to achieve a very high savings rate in order to get to millionaire status by such a young age. And then once you hit the financial independence point it's important to be diligent and mindful to keep expenses in check so as not to erode the assets that will fund your entire retirement (which is a lot longer, based on the early start). I saw how fabulously that FIRE could really work for Tara specifically. She was the youngest client I had with a level of wealth that put her well on track to achieving FIRE status.

This meeting was the perfect opportunity to share this amazing revelation with her that she would be able to retire in *seven* years. As we took our seats in the booth, I started by explaining the FIRE concept and illustrated how the numbers worked out for her specifically based on where she was at. She could retire with over $1 million in the bank. The income generated from the investments could be used to fund her living expenses. And by sticking to that yearly rate of drawing on the income, it would ensure she didn't draw down the principal amount to fund a nice and long retirement.

I was all smiles as I showed the projections over the next several years. And then it was time for the big moment, where I revealed how she would be able to retire with over a million by thirty.

Ta-dahhh!

I imagined the conversation playing out with *big* excitement. Maybe her leaping up from her chair, or perhaps letting out a tiny squeal . . . But I got nothing. She sat there looking completely unfazed. Being thrown off by her complete indifference, I waited a moment in case she was still processing what I had said. Seconds passed and still nothing.

To break the silence, I asked, "Soooo, what do you think?"

"That's cool to know, but not really what I had in mind," she replied.

I was perplexed. *She didn't want to be a millionaire and be free by the age of thirty!*

Perhaps sensing my confusion, she elaborated, "I'm excited to continue to build my wealth, but I want to aim for more. I want an abundance of money so I don't ever have to feel guilty about my expenses in retirement. And realistically, I love what I do, so I don't want to stop working anytime soon."

Everything she was saying made perfect sense because it was exactly what she wanted. She was expressing her unique money goals. I was embarrassed that I had tried to push a strategy upon her that wasn't aligned with them. It was a powerful *ah-ha moment* that taught me how important it is to ask, to listen, and to seek to understand before I can provide any strategies or solutions because, again, each person is so different.

Embracing your money uniqueness will not always be easy. But in the end, it's absolutely worth it. You're not on this earth to live anyone's life but your own. Stay true to what you want, especially when it comes to your money.

TAKING ACTION

And now as promised, it's time to embrace your own money uniqueness. For this exercise, I encourage you to write out/journal your responses to the questions below. These are a few prompts to get you focused on *you* and what *you* desire. But feel free to include any additional money dreams and ideas that come up for you during this exercise (and don't skip the details!):

- What's important about money to you?
- What does being wealthy mean to you?
- Do you want to be a millionaire? A multimillionaire?
- What is your ideal living situation? Is home ownership important to you? Do you desire a vacation property or second home?
- Is travel and adventure a goal for you? And if so, how many trips would you ideally want to go on each year?
- Is there a particular purchase that you would like to be able to splurge on?
- What is your ideal career? And what is your desired income goal for the work you do?
- At what age would you like to achieve financial independence?
- What does the ideal retirement look like for you? Are you still doing some form of work during your retirement years? Or have you completely stopped working?
- If you have children do you have goals for assisting them in their early adult years (i.e. postsecondary education funding or a house down payment)?

PART 2

BUILDING YOUR MONEY MUSCLES

CHAPTER 6

BE OPEN TO LEARNING

YOU DUG DEEP and did the inner work. Congrats to you! Going within to face your past money stuff isn't easy but it's essential to moving forward on this journey to financial confidence. So I hope you're feeling lighter and ready for this next stage which is all about building your money muscle.

The book title *Make Money Your Thing!* is very important, as it's how I answer women when they put themselves down about their money abilities. What I hear over and over again when I speak to women about their finances are comments such as:

I'm not good with money.
I'm not good at math.
I'm not a numbers person.

And of course, the dreaded phrase that inspired me to write this book:

Money isn't my thing.

If you've said these things you aren't alone. But know that self-criticism isn't serving you. By saying these phrases, you're essentially giving up. Maybe giving up before even *trying* to make "money your thing." The above declarations don't offer any optimism or hope and won't foster a positive relationship with your money. They may actually be harming you, by closing off the possibilities. If you've ever found yourself saying anything along the lines of the above, I'm suggesting in the kindest way possible—*please, please, please* STOP RIGHT NOW. Do yourself a massive favor by removing these phrases from your vocab for good.

Instead, here's an alternative. A new path, a new approach to your money. One that's empowering. And even quite simple.

Simple? How simple, you may be asking . . .

Simple because all it involves is one action. The act of learning something new. That's right, the alternative is this—you can learn money skills.

You *can* make money your thing!

You've already been learning your whole life. From the time you learned to crawl, then to walk, to read and write, to play a sport, or to create a work of art. And learning about money is no different. It takes time and practice.

Please don't give up before trying. If numbers and equations look like hieroglyphics and cause your head to spin, that's okay! Because that's how all learning starts. There's no defeat in that; it's simply the beginning of learning something new.

It's time to stop hiding behind the excuse of money not being your thing (or some other version of the phrase). Just because it hasn't been your thing up until now doesn't mean you can't learn it and *make money your thing*! There's no time like the present to change this, and I'm assuming that's exactly why you're reading this book in the first place.

Nobody begins anything as an expert. At one point, driving wasn't my thing. The first time I got behind the steering wheel of a car, I was terrified. Everything felt foreign and unnatural. But each time my mom came to pick me up after my shift at Dairy Queen before getting my license, I begged her to let me drive home so I could practice because I *wanted* to learn. I wanted to get better so I could drive solo. I had my learner's permit and the only way I was going to be able to get my license exam was with practice.

Sure enough, every trip home progressively got easier. Each time I drove it became a bit more comfortable, and my mom looked a bit less terrified. In fact, I got so comfortable driving that when I saved up to buy my first vehicle at the age of sixteen; I was unfazed by the stick shift, which I had *no* idea how to drive *yet*. But I had the confidence that I could learn. I stalled at every single traffic light and stop sign for the first few days, which was extremely embarrassing, but by the end of the week, I was shifting gears with ease.

With this same beginner's mindset and openness, I'm confident that you can grow your money and investing knowledge.

And for those of you who still aren't sold on the idea, I want you to know that I appreciate that money might feel very foreign to you—like "driving a stick shift" kind of foreign. Most people aren't introduced to any money or personal finance topics throughout their entire formal education experience.

Unfortunately, financial literacy has not been integrated across the board into the standard school curriculum. This means that from kindergarten through to high school graduation, you may not have participated in a single class or lesson about money. And what is even more alarming is that if you went on to attend college—financial literacy education was likely still overlooked.

How crazy is that?

Money is part of your everyday life. You earn it and use it to buy stuff and pay bills. Yet it still isn't a skill you're taught to develop throughout your formal education.

This means that when you're all grown up and begin earning an income, you may not know about saving, investing, budgeting, or filing taxes. Instead, you are left floundering to figure it out on the fly, feeling like you're drinking from a firehose. It's too much. The feelings are overwhelming.

What wasn't offered in school becomes a crash course in your adult years, called "figure it out, or go broke." Not the optimal condition to learn anything new, especially not when it comes to something as important as your money. These are tricky topics with lots of moving parts. And having to learn it all in a hurry could put you at risk of making poor financial decisions and suffering a sizable loss.

The firehose method isn't ideal when it comes to mastering your finances. The best way to learn about your money is gradually and progressively, by starting with the basics and building upon that. Ideally, you want to be able to take it in as bite-sized chunks, not eating the whole darn cake. It needs to be done at your own pace.

It's fair to say that *yes*; with all these factors working against you, money may not have been your thing up until this point. And with good reason. You may have gone your entire life without learning a single thing about money. And now, you're expected to be an expert overnight and do all the right things with it.

But I'm here to proclaim—that's not realistic.

Learning takes time and practice, no matter what you're learning. Money skills aren't genetic—to believe that some people are born with them, while others don't inherit the genes. Anyone can learn about money, even the math haters!

Give yourself grace and be patient about your financial literacy.

If you're open to the idea of making money your thing but are resistant to being the newbie, I get that too (as a recovering perfectionist myself). You might be uncomfortable at the prospect of messing up or looking dumb as a "grown up." If you're feeling a bit rusty, let me give you a reminder of what it looks and feels like to learn.

This past summer, I implemented nonnegotiable evening walks as part of my self-care routine. One evening, while following my regular path around the neighborhood, there was a young girl who looked to be about nine years old on a foot-powered scooter. As I walked by, she did the same short loop down the sidewalk onto the road, back up onto the sidewalk, and then would turn around and do it all over again. I wondered why she kept doing it over and over again; it was awfully repetitive.

And then the lightbulb of realization followed—oh, she was practicing!

Yes, that's correct; the concept of practicing to develop a skill was so foreign to me that it took me a moment for my brain to comprehend what I was seeing. But unfolding right before my eyes was a girl destined to excel at scootering as she mastered that loop, even the hop at the end. Practice makes perfect indeed!

There's an underlying expectation that when you hit a certain age, you must know it all, and for anything that was missed, it's too late. That's a dangerous belief—to put an expiry date on learning something new. It's the reason many women who don't currently feel confident about money have decided their futures have been decided. That their relationship with money is set. And that money will never be their thing.

But it's not too late; you always have the ability to learn.

I recently had a conversation with a woman named Emma who was given my contact from a divorce support group. She shared that her ex had taken the lead over their finances during their twenty-five-year marriage. Now that she was in her fifties and in charge of her own finances for the first time, she felt lost. I asked her to share her short-, medium-, and long-term goals for her money. And I broke down the steps that we would take to get her there. I assured her that although it seemed like a lot and might sound overwhelming in that moment, there was no pending final exam. It was about taking it one step at a time, and for her the first step was opening her own individual accounts. It's never too late and there's always an opportunity to make money your thing at any age or stage of life.

You *have to* learn at every age. Don't let your ego get the best of you and decide, "Well, if I don't know it by now, I suppose I never will." Education takes time, and you might need to be exposed to certain concepts over and over again before they make sense. But that repetition, like the scooter girl looping the same path, is called practice, and it's an essential part of your learning journey.

This is something I've often reminded the participants who take my Investing 101 course, to be patient and not expect to leave the one-day course as a money guru. To accept they might have to hear or read about the same money topic several times until it's absorbed as knowledge. But that's completely okay because if this is the very first time being exposed to it, practice and repetition will help it sink in. In fact, when I taught the course again this past fall, there was a woman sitting in the front row who was so recognizable, but I couldn't put my finger on where I had met her. Finally, on the lunch break it hit me—she had already taken this course the year before.

This made me giddy for two reasons. First, she must actually enjoy my teaching if she opted to sit through it for another eight hours! And second, she'd truly embraced my opening remarks about being patient and accepting that it could take some repetition before the concepts made sense. She had enrolled herself again as a refresher to what she'd learned the year before. And she had no shame in doing so. She participated, asked questions, and approached me at the end to thank me and tell me she enjoyed taking the course for the second time. She's an inspiring example of a woman dedicated to being confident about her money.

I'm hopeful that like this woman you too are ready to make money your thing—you are reading this book, after all! Now that you're ready, it's time to get going—let's talk about how you can commit to learning to build your money muscle.

Here are some ideas you can try right away:

Talk Money with Family and Friends

People don't chat about money enough. Feelings of shame and vulnerability can make talking about it scary and uncomfortable. But communicating about it is how you increase your financial literacy. When you talk about financial concepts with people you know and trust, you create an opportunity to pick up ideas and learn new things.

When it comes to money chit-chat, you don't have to get overly detailed and share the dollars and cents but, with someone you trust, you can get curious and ask for their ideas and suggestions.

I had a pivotal money conversation about pay raises with my best friend Denise in my early working years. At the time, I was in a job where the pay was crap. I talked to Denise about her earnings and asked her for advice about approaching my boss about a raise. She was very open to sharing what had worked for her when she had a similar conversation with her boss.

I was grateful for her listening ear but on top of that, her advice was exactly what I needed to prepare myself for marching into that office, head held high knowing what I was deserving of. I'm forever grateful to Denise for the pay pep talk because I got that raise! And I didn't puke or pass out in the process. Talking openly, rather than keeping it inside, was the best thing I could've done. You never have to be a lone wolf when it comes to your money. The people you love can offer a safe space to share openly and learn from.

Reading Bites

Like the power of compounding growth, I'm a strong believer in the power of compounding knowledge. For people who are looking to build their financial smarts, I suggest committing to reading one finance or money-related article per week. It's simple and realistic. It doesn't require a major time commitment—try simply swapping out a single session of social media scrolling each week. Even the busiest person can spare five to ten minutes per week. Articles tend to be short and sweet, so you're limiting yourself to taking in a bite-sized nugget of new information.

It's crucial to be patient with yourself on this learning journey. Just *one* article per week is a fabulous start. And from this new weekly habit, a natural compounding growth of knowledge will follow. The first piece might go completely over your head. But with each new read, you'll start to get better acquainted with concepts and jargon as you see them repeated. And if you're more of an auditory learner, you can opt to listen to a money- or finance-related podcast instead. There are so many fabulous podcasts available freely. So, if it's more convenient to listen on the go, or if you prefer the audio experience, this is a perfect alternative.

Money Books

There's an abundance of personal finance and investing books available. And I'm so proud of you for taking the time to read this one right now! Articles are a great way to build your general knowledge and stay up to date on any relevant changes, but if you're looking for a deeper dive into a specific money or investing topic, there's likely a book for that.

Leah, a client who was very eager to build her financial literacy, asked me for recommendations—my favorite books about investing. I gave her a few suggestions to start and then sent her more over the next several months. When we got together for a review meeting, she told me that she had recently started a money book club with several of her girlfriends—one where all selections had to be investing or money-related topics. This was a brilliant idea. Not only were they sharpening their financial literacy skills, but they were doing it in a comfortable and welcoming way. They were learning together, to make it less daunting, and more engaging and fun.

School Yourself

As I shared earlier on, there's a good chance that there were no investing or money-related courses at your school. But there's no time like the present to enroll in one now. There are plenty of options for investing seminars and courses, in person and online. For in-person events, take a look at the offerings at your local college, university, or continuing education programs and keep an eye out for courses on money management or investing.

And remember, you don't have to do this alone. Consider taking the course with a friend or family member. As mentioned, I teach an Investing 101 course and there have been plenty of times that couples and friends attended together. There have also been several parents attending the course with their teens. I *love* seeing parents encourage their children to learn these concepts. What better investment in your child's future? And, it's saving you, in the long run, to encourage financial independence so your kiddos aren't dependent on the bank of Mom forever.

It's never too late to learn, and encouraging the next generation to get started on the right foot is powerful. If there are no such options available in your area, consider taking your search online. With more and more programs moving online, you're sure to find a virtual option. Just because you didn't have these classes in school, doesn't mean you can't do them now.

These are a few simple ideas to build that money muscle, but the key is to do what works for you and what is engaging and maybe even fun! It doesn't have to fill you with dread like going for your routine physical. Focus on what you can easily incorporate into your schedule. It all starts by getting out of your own way and no longer hiding behind your excuses. You'll succeed if you're open and willing to learn because it's never too late to learn something new. It will take time and practice to build up your financial literacy bank, especially if you're learning the concepts for the first time, but you'll be amazed by the results of compounding knowledge.

TAKING ACTION

Commit to one act of growing your knowledge on a money/personal finance topic (listen to a podcast, take a course, follow a money expert on your social networks, subscribe to a newsletter, finish this book, etc.).

CHAPTER 7

MONEY AWARENESS (PART 1)

RECENTLY MY DAUGHTER Ivy and I took a vacation to California and, of course, Disney was the highlight of our trip. My fellow high achievers reading this who've been to Disneyland, I'm sure, can agree that as soon as you enter the park you're on a mission to get in as many rides as possible. There's no time to waste. Especially if you buy the Park Hopper pass, giving access to *both* parks, then you have no excuse not to get those double digits on your ride count!

Thankfully, technology has your back and you can now use the trusty park map located within the Disney app on your phone as your advisor. The app gives you updated wait times for all the rides. As you set out to navigate your best walking path to the ride of choice based on proximity and wait time (I'm such a planner), there's a pop-up on your screen that asks to use your *current location*. This same pop-up appears when using your phone's GPS or the map app—you can't expect to get directions to your desired location if you don't (or your phone doesn't) know your current location.

You can't start *any* journey without first knowing where you stand. All journeys begin this way. As you make money your thing, this is also true for your financial journey. You first must know where you stand. Money awareness is the key to finding the "current location" of your finances.

This chapter will provide you with the essential tools you'll need to develop your money awareness. Establishing money awareness is the starting point to working toward your financial dreams (your desired destination).

Here are three basic but very important questions to find your current money location:

1. How much money do you have today?
2. How much money do you earn each month/year?
3. How much money do you spend each month/year?

Pretty basic, right? But most people don't have the answers. So know it's completely okay if you don't know yet, but the goal of this chapter is to get you there!

Having this insight is an important piece of your overall financial life. Money awareness is the input into all financial planning and decisions when you're goal setting. You can't set out to reach any goal if you don't know your current location because you'll most likely get lost, take many wrong turns, end up somewhere completely different, or spend an entire day at Disney with more blisters on your feet than rides under your belt.

Maybe your primary goal is to have no credit card debt in three years, pay off your mortgage in ten years, retire at age fifty-five, or buy a McDonald's franchise (anyone else with me on this one?).

These and any other goals are all fabulous, but you'll never get there if you don't know where you currently stand.

It all starts by taking an inventory of what you have now, then coupling that with knowing what you're adding, and spending on an ongoing basis. These inputs combined provide the money awareness you'll need to pinpoint your starting location.

Let's start with the first question: How much money do you have today?

The best tool to provide you with a measure of how much money you have is a net worth statement. This might be new to you, if so that's completely fine; it's not as fancy as it sounds. Think of a net worth statement as your wealth snapshot that lists everything you own and everything you owe. And since I also think it sounds better, I'll stick to calling it your wealth snapshot . . . unless I forget, but hopefully I don't.

Your wealth snapshot is like looking at the balance in your bank account—but it combines your entire wealth picture into that number, rather than just reporting your checking account balance. Unfortunately, this one number isn't as easy to retrieve as your bank balance. Simply signing into the app won't get you there. You'll have to do a bit of work to gather all the inputs.

To create your wealth snapshot, first, you'll list everything you own. And then separately, list everything you owe. I will go into further detail about what to include in each of those lists in a moment. But to keep it organized in your head think of it as two columns, or lists, one labeled "Assets" (what you own) and the other "Liabilities" (what you owe).

To answer the first question, you will have to do a bit of math to combine those two columns. We aren't talking algebra or calculus.

Just plain addition and subtraction, and unlike when you first learned math, there are no rules against using a calculator. I love calculators!

Adding everything in your assets column (what you own) and then separately adding everything in your liabilities column (what you owe) will get you a total for each. Once those are both summed up separately take the assets number and minus the liabilities from it, and then you have the answer to question #1. And if my explanation made your brain hurt, this is what the math looks like:

Total Assets – Total Liabilities = Your Wealth Snapshot

Based on the calculation above, you can see that if assets exceed liabilities, your number will be positive (you own more than you owe). Conversely, if liabilities are greater than assets you'll have a negative number. This means that what you owe is more than what you own. There is a very real possibility that it could be a negative number, and there's no need to panic if so. It all depends on your unique situation and stage of life. But a negative number that continues to get bigger (even more into the negative) is not sustainable. Ideally, you'll want to see the number gradually increasing, which supports the premise of building wealth. Remember this is a no-judgment zone. It's simply an awareness exercise with the main goal of answering the question, "How much money do you have today?" Or, "Where do you currently stand with your finances?"

How do you track your wealth snapshot? You can use a spreadsheet, a fancy notebook, or a ledger, or write it on a napkin. It's up to you!

Now let's breakdown what will be included in the assets versus liability columns.

Assets (What You Own)

For assets, think of this as cash or any items of value that can be converted or sold for cash. Assets can include bank/investment accounts or physical assets you own such as a home. The most common examples of assets are:

- Cash in bank accounts
- Balances in investment accounts (including all savings and retirement accounts)
- The value of your home (approximate current resale value)
- Personal property you own

When it comes to personal property only include items that you could sell at or above what you paid for them. Not things that someone can bargain you down on or can find for free on Facebook Marketplace. Some examples could be jewelry, collectors' items, and art. I suggest you leave out vehicles in this category because they tend to lose their value quickly. As the saying goes, a car is worth less the minute you drive it off the lot—which means it doesn't pass the test for holding value or going up in price.

Liabilities (What You Owe)

In the liability column include everything you owe. Examples are:

- Mortgage balance
- Car loan
- Student loan

- Any other personal loans
- Balance on credit line
- Credit card balances

Once you have listed all assets and all liabilities add up the total of each column, to give you total assets and total liabilities. And then you bring back that lovely equation I included earlier on:

Total Assets – Total Liabilities = Your Wealth Snapshot

This activity might not be as fun as a trip to Disney, but knowing where you stand is how you make the dream vacations a reality. If you only do one activity from this book I would recommend it be this task of calculating your wealth snapshot number, so you have an inventory of exactly what you have and what you owe. Included below are a few examples in case I've completely lost you. Let's walk through the process of creating Jane and Emily's wealth snapshots:

What's Jane's story—she recently graduated, started her career, and is ready to take stock of where she stands:

- Some savings in the bank of $2,500
- Employer retirement plan of $6,500
- She wants to do some investing and holds a direct investment account with $3,500
- Has $3,000 remaining on her student loan
- Credit card balance of $1,250
- Financed her car and still owes $5,500

Now comes the journaling, scrap piece of paper, or spreadsheet for the math step:

JANE'S WEALTH SNAPSHOT

Assets		Liabilities	
Savings Account	$2,500	Student Loan	$3,000
Retirement Plan	$6,500	Credit Card	$1,250
Investments	$3,500	Car Financing	$5,500
Total Assets	$12,500	Total Liabilities	$9,750

Total Assets – Total Liabilities = Wealth Snapshot
$12,500 – $9,750 = $2,750
Jane's current wealth snapshot total is $2,750.

And now for Emily who is in her forties and established in her career as a lawyer:

- Has a healthy emergency account of $35,000
- Savings account balance of $10,000
- She has a tax-sheltered investment account and a retirement investment account, combined total of $125,000
- Owns her home and based on recent sales in her community she thinks she could sell it for $495,000
- Did some home renos and owes $35,000 on her line of credit
- She financed her car and still owes $15,500
- Outstanding mortgage balance of $325,000

EMILY'S WEALTH SNAPSHOT

Assets		Liabilities	
Emergency Account	$35,000	Line of Credit	$35,000
Savings Account	$10,000	Car Financing	$15,500
Investments	$125,000	Mortgage Balance	$325,000
Home Value	$495,000		
Total Assets	**$665,000**	**Total Liabilities**	**$375,500**

Total Assets—Total Liabilities = Wealth Snapshot

$665,000 - $375,500 = $289,500

Emily's current wealth snapshot total is $289,500.

Above we've captured where Jane and Emily stand, their current location and the answer to the first question—"How much money do you have today?"

Keep in mind that this total measures your money inventory at a specific point in time. The number can and will change. When you add to savings, pay off loans, or make mortgage payments this number will go up or down, like the balance in your bank account changes when you withdraw cash, make a purchase, or when it's payday.

This means you'll want to update these numbers on an ongoing basis (so technology might be preferred for tracking over a flimsy napkin). But you don't have to update as often as something like your bank balance is updated. To keep your wealth snapshot current I suggest as a minimum you aim to update once or twice per year, or with major money events (like when you receive that well-deserved bonus at work). But if you want to keep a closer pulse on things, feel free to check in with your money more often.

A word of caution: this exercise is about creating the awareness so you can know where you stand in your financial life. It's not about judging your worth based on the number. Doing the work to create the awareness is something to be proud of and celebrate, no matter where you stand today.

This wealth snapshot was a game changer for my client Grace (I'll share more about her in Chapter 14). To summarize, Grace longed to be a millionaire by age forty. The planning we did—to find out exactly what she had to do to get there—wouldn't have been possible if we didn't know her starting location. And now she's more than halfway there!

Once you've created your own wealth snapshot it can serve as the starting point for your desired destinations. Maybe you're saving for a down payment for your dream home in five years. Or maybe you have a specific money target like Grace did—for instance, get to a net worth of $500,000 in ten years. If your number was negative to start then maybe your focus is on getting it to positive territory within a certain time frame. The possibilities are endless on what you may be inspired to work toward, but the journey starts by knowing where you are starting from.

You've done some heavy lifting in this chapter by learning the best tool to answer the first question "How much money do you have today?" But the work isn't quite done with your money awareness, so let's complete the missing pieces to answer the two remaining questions in the next chapter.

TAKING ACTION

If you took the time to complete your own wealth snapshot during the chapter then you're a superstar and have already done the assignment. Congrats!

And if you haven't done it yet, now is the time! Take inventory of your wealth by completing your own wealth snapshot.

- Start with the dividing your page/spreadsheet into the two columns and then list all your assets and liabilities.
- Get out the calculator and add up each column, so you have one total for each (total assets *and* total liabilities).
- Lastly, input your totals into the lovely equation to get your number

Total Assets – Total Liabilities = Wealth Snapshot.

If this assignment feels a bit overwhelming at this time you can start by building the outline. Create your columns—assets and liabilities—and write down the items applicable to each. For instance, maybe under the asset category you list: home, retirement account, savings account, for the time being. And then come back to fill in the numbers when you are ready to complete the equation.

CHAPTER 8

MONEY AWARENESS (PART 2)

NOW IT'S TIME TO ADDRESS the next two questions introduced at the start of the previous chapter, and complete the picture of your money awareness:

How much money do you earn each month/year?
How much money do you spend each month/year?

A handy tool to tackle the above would be a budget. But the word *budget* isn't very sexy, I know. In fact, you may be cringing at the thought of reading on, now that I've used the *B word*. But please give me a chance to put a positive spin on it. The purpose of a budget is to follow your cash flow—money coming in *AND* money going out.

Still boring, I know.

But let's put some perspective on the value of it. A budget shows you *where your hard-earned money is going.* If you hate budgets and want nothing to do with them, then spending without one sends the message—

I don't want to know where my money is going.

I suspect this doesn't sit well with you, or at least not anymore, not now that you've decided to make money your thing! Don't let your money sneak away from you. Budgeting helps you babysit your money, and keeping tabs on your cash means you know exactly where it's going.

I might have captured your interest with this whole keeping tabs on your money concept. But you may still have some objections. I hear them all the time.

Budgets are _____:

- Time-consuming
- Complicated
- For people who like math
- Boring
- Unnecessary
- Restrictive

Confession time. I admit, budgets themselves may not be fun, but our mindset around them can be. My advice here is inspired by the late author and speaker, Wayne Dyer (one of my favorites in the self-development/spiritual growth field), who explained that by looking at things differently, the things themselves can change. That's exactly what I propose you do about budgeting (thank you, Wayne): start looking at it differently. Let's start by offering alternative perspectives to the above myths and excuses about budgeting.

Budgets are time-consuming: Life gets busy, and you have a pile of tasks competing for your time. As a single parent and business owner myself, I know firsthand how busy life can get, and how grateful I am for the conveniences in life (Amazon Prime and Uber Eats). But the time commitment to keeping a budget can be deceiving. For most people, even an hour or two per month is enough to keep your budget up to date. The length of one episode of the *Real Housewives*, and you could be on your way to being the master of your cash flow, no rich husband necessary.

And for the perspective shift, instead of avoiding it based on the time it takes, think of what the time spent on your budget could be worth. By spending some time tracking your cash flow you might discover cost savings or be able to reduce unnecessary expenses—a return on your time that can add up to cold, hard cash.

Budgets are too difficult or complicated: This is an easy trap to fall into. But it's simply not true. There really is nothing ultra-complicated about doing a budget; it uses a combination of addition and subtraction that you learned in grade school. And remember, the use of calculators is permitted and encouraged.

Making a budget might initially feel challenging if you've never done one before, but that's because it's new and unfamiliar. New things have a tendency to scare us off like you read about in Chapter 6 and, as adults, we forget what it means to learn something new. But once the initial discomfort passes, this new habit will become much easier.

The good news is, there aren't specific rules to follow when you're doing your budget and nobody is going to be grading you on how you did. Learning something new can also be an exciting time. It's empowering to dive into unknown territory and come out of it with new skills and abilities. It might just remind you that you're capable of anything! Learning never stops and trying new things is a great way to keep your brain sharp. So jump in and get a little uncomfortable.

Budgets are boring: Okay, if the act of doing your budget sounds worse than a colonoscopy—I get it. For the longest time, I ranked budgets on the entertainment scale somewhere between folding laundry and cleaning toilets. But that all changed in the early days of my career when I met with a young woman named Veronica. She had a spectacular energy about her and radiated positivity. When we sat down to discuss her finances, she was eager to share her budget. And once I saw it, I understood why. It was by far the most impressive budget I'd ever seen.

Created on legal-sized paper, it unfolded into a larger poster-sized banner. It was covered in colorful labels and was split into categories with headings that jumped off the page with bolded fonts. I was stunned as she proudly laid it across my desk. The details, effort, and passion she put into it amazed me. Her excitement was contagious. I wasn't just impressed, I was inspired! That evening I went home and sat down to do an updated version of my own budget, knowing mine too was worthy of a far greater effort than I had given it in the past. It deserved some color, bolded titles, funky fonts, and a little extra time and attention. Budgets can be boring, but if you change the way you look at them they can also be a fun project. Get the Veronica vibe going for your budget. Make it an extravagant event by putting on some tunes as you work, get your partner involved, or do it with a friend, and get creative.

Budgets are redundant; I already have a rough estimate of my spending: This is the go-to approach for many people I chat with about their spending. They take the largest expenses they have each month (mortgage, utilities, insurance, etc.) sum them up in their head, and guesstimate their budget. They might even round up the numbers a bit, figuring that gives them some wiggle room for anything they missed.

When I come across people using this estimating approach, I encourage them to go through a complete month of expenses in detail—to double-check their accuracy. Guess what? Most people are terrible at approximating what they spend. If the activity was akin to guessing the number of jelly beans in the jar, they might be guessing 63 when the answer is 1042. Not even close. This approach misses out on all the small expenses, and those little buggers can really add up. These include stopping at the convenience store when you're parched for a five-dollar bottled water, paying for subscriptions that seem like nothing on their own but combined are equivalent to a car payment, and don't get me started on the takeout—which makes fast food no longer seem like the cheap option.

I get it; it's very tempting to do a rough estimate version of your budget, for the simplicity and speed. If you pay your bills each month the assumption is you know how much you spend. But trust me— you don't. And now to change the perspective, guesstimating your budget isn't providing you with valuable insight into your spending. You deserve to know the truth about your money by taking an honest look at how much you actually spend. And you might even be surprised what you find out if it turns out there's more left over than you originally thought.

Budgets are too restrictive: A budget doesn't have to be akin to going on a money diet. The act of simply doing your budget doesn't require you to stop all discretionary spending and cut back on the extras. Because what is life without dinners out for the endless salad and breadsticks from the Olive Garden? When you see the results of your budget, you may choose to make some changes or adjustments to your spending habits. But that really depends on you and your money goals.

Now to shift your perspective—remember that you're always in the driver's seat when it comes to your money. A budget cannot tell you what you can and can't spend money on.

The act of doing your budget is an awareness exercise. Be grateful to your budget for providing insight into your spending, to help you make important decisions on anything that stands out that you might want to change, or for what it simply reaffirms. Give yourself permission to skip cooking every so often so you can enjoy those breadsticks.

I earn more than enough; I don't need a budget: I would love to tell you that when you attain a certain level of wealth you enter the exclusive "Budget Freedom" club, but that isn't the case. Budgets serve as important cash-tracking tools and add value no matter where you are in your financial journey, whether you're just getting started in your career or if you're experienced and at the top of your earnings game.

I work with a lot of clients that have received pay raises that coincide with their years of experience. What can happen when people don't have an awareness of what they spend versus earn is that they can easily and quickly adjust their spending upward each time they get a salary bump. What may start as buying Starbucks every day instead of brewing your coffee at home, and springing for the premium gas can easily snowball to flying first class, a collection of designer bags, and properties that you didn't even remember you owned (yes, I'm talking about you, Kris Jenner).

Budgets aren't only for those who are scraping by. A multimillionaire client I work with still tracks her spending every month and raves about staying on track with her financial priorities.

A budget can provide valuable insight into your finances at all stages of your life, and you will never be too successful to reap the benefits.

Now is not the best time: This is an excuse that comes up in all elements of people's financial lives. The idea of putting things off for a better time. Perhaps you've decided to put off the budget until you get that raise, or pay off your credit card, or when your mortgage is lower, or when your kids are older. Whatever the reason, there will always be something to justify pushing it out into the future.

By putting off doing your budget you're wasting precious time to build an understanding of your spending habits. Every year, I take a good look at my budget. This past year, I canceled my satellite radio, Spotify, my extra Dropbox storage, and called the phone company to bundle my internet and phone, netting $250/month in savings. That equates to over $3,000/year that I was spending unnecessarily. That will really pump up my retirement savings fund.

And now it's time for the perspective shift—there's no time like the present to do your budget. Like a treasure hunt into the depths of your couch cushions, you might even find some extra cash. Even with a big life change on the horizon, no problem. You can still do your budget now, and then go back and check in on it afterward to see if any adjustments are in order.

They really aren't so bad, after all. Budgeting empowers you to track your cash flow so you're using your money wisely, spending it on buying things you want or need, and giving less of it to services you've outgrown and never use.

Now that we've worked on changing the way you look at budgets, it's time to get started on creating yours!

My Hottest Tips For Budgeting

Let's first break budgets down into two types—past and future. Past looks in the rearview to show your spending habits. The future budget is focused forward on your money goals.

Just as it sounds, the past budget calculates income versus expenses in the previous months. It helps create an awareness of what you earn and spend each month. To create your past budget, start by picking a previous month that represents a typical month of spending (avoid a holiday month when the cash is flowing a little more generously). Once you've selected a recent past month, gather all transactions over that entire month.

This is where keeping things simple comes in handy. If you have multiple bank accounts and credit cards gather transactions from each of those payment methods. Quick note when you're gathering transactions from a past month: don't forget about yearly or quarterly payments. Although they might not be listed in the transaction history for that month, you don't want to miss capturing these in your expenses. For example, if you pay for your car insurance on a yearly basis take the annual premium and divide it by twelve to get the monthly equivalent. Gather *everything*, and don't forget any of those sneaky little purchases.

There are different ways for gathering and sorting your information. I find using the computer the quickest method as it makes it easier to combine the data and make changes. There are also budget templates that you can grab from the internet. But if the template doesn't feel fitting for your circumstances or you find there are a lot of categories included that aren't applicable, then no pressure to follow it. When it comes to creating your past budget there's no right or wrong answer. Do what works for you. (Remember it can be fun, creative, and innovative!)

Be a money detective, and find every transaction from the first day of the month until the last date. Once each transaction is listed for the month, separate those that are income (money coming in) from expenses (money going out). You can then add up all the income amounts to get your total monthly income, and separately you can add up all the expenses to get your total monthly expenses.

Guess what? You just answered the remaining two questions from the start of the chapter:

How much money do you earn? (money coming in)
How much money do you spend? (money going out)

The list of all your expenses for the month is probably relatively long and full of a hodge-podge of bills and things you've bought over the month. Now is a good time to Marie Kondo your expenses. A deeper level of understanding your spending comes from organizing the expenses. You can sort and categorize each monthly expense to uncover where the bulk of your money is being spent. Here are ideas of categories you could use for sorting your expenses:

1. Housing
2. Transportation

3. Serious Food
4. Takeout and treats
5. The boring category (such as utilities)
6. Insurance
7. Health and wellness
8. Yours to keep—saving and investing
9. Debt payments
10. Style
11. Entertainment
12. Travel and adventure
13. Miscellaneous

But you don't have to categorize in any particular way, get innovative and come up with the labels and categories that seem fitting to you. Like organizing your home, where you choose to categorize each entry is up to you. But the important part is having a system that works and is repeatable, so you can actually remember where you put things. Once you've created the categories, add each expense for the month to its spot. When all expenses have been assigned you can total up the amount in each section.

Your detective work is done; you've now solved the mystery of where your money goes. And which category you spend the most in each month. For those that like to dive deeper into the details, you can do even more with this information. For instance, you can calculate the percentage you spend in each category every month to get an understanding of your spending ratios. Perhaps you find you spend 5% more eating out than you do on grocery store trips each month. Again, the past budget is a look into the rearview to develop an awareness of your income versus expenses. Say goodbye to phrases like "Where does all my money go?" or "I have no idea how much money I spend."

If in doing this exercise, you discovered that you spend more than you make—well then it's even better that you did this now! Spending more than you earn isn't sustainable in the long run. The only way to keep it up is by using debt or dwindling your savings. It also doesn't give you the ability to build your wealth, which relies on accumulating savings.

Before we move on to the forward-looking budget, let's summarize the steps above for your past budget:

1. Select a previous month of typical spending.
2. Gather all transactions from that month. Don't forget to include the monthly portion of annual or quarterly payments.
3. Capture every transaction for the month from all methods of payments.
4. Separate income from expenses.
5. Add up the income entries (if you have multiple in the month).
6. Add up the expenses.
7. Are you spending more than you earn?
8. Create categories to sort the expenses.
9. Allocate each expense item to a category.
10. Add the expenses of each category to get a monthly total for each—i.e., Transportation (including gas, car payment, car insurance) = $650/month.
11. Feel free to do some extra analysis on your categories to get a better understanding of spending habits and where the majority of your money goes.

And now for the next budgeting tool. Your future budget. Or feel free to rename it anything you like (some ideas to get the creative juices flowing: *Prosperity Plan, Money Boss Budget, Empowered Earnings, Cash Flow Fortune, Raining Riches, etc.*).

This is all about you being empowered to take control of where your money goes, and that includes what you choose to call it; I call mine "Empire Building." Creating a future budget allows you to get intentional with your money. Instead of simply calculating what you already spent in the past, it's about being proactive and deciding where you want your money to go. If there was anything that surprised you about where your money is being spent, now is your chance to make changes and incorporate goals. If you were happy with the results of your past spending, that's awesome. And if that's the case maybe the goal is to keep a good thing going.

The future budget is based on what you discovered from your past budget. So unfortunately you can't skip to planning for the future without working out the past numbers first. Think of this exercise as getting to design your best budget. You can use the same categories that you created for your backward-looking budget, but for this exercise you get to decide the ideal amount you want to spend in each. You are creating a plan for how much and where you want to see your money going. Perhaps (like me) you discovered you spend far more at McDonald's than you realized and you want to scale back on that expense going forward.

When you're creating your future plan, be specific and realistic. A client named Alice, who is a busy professional, often opted to buy her lunches to save time. On really intense days when she worked well into the evening, she also ended up ordering dinner to her office. When she went through this exercise, she was shocked to discover her "Eating Out" category was close to $1,000 each month. She had no idea the expense was that high, and she didn't want to be eating away that much of her hard-earned cash.

The awareness motivated her to make a change, and her ultimate goal was to get her eating-out expense down to $250/monthly. She knew this would be a challenge, so she aimed to gradually reduce it over the next several months until she reached her goal. She was excited to make the change and planned on splitting the $750 per monthly savings between her vacation account (for her love of travel), and the other half toward her financial freedom goal.

When it comes to your cash flow, the goal is to feel in control and happy about your spending each month. Feeling like you have no idea where your money goes or that you're at the mercy of your bills can be very disempowering. Developing your future budget will help you get intentional about your spending.

Creating the best budget for you isn't a one-and-done task. For best results, you'll want to check in to ensure you're sticking to your targets. Try reviewing at the end of the month to see how you did. Or, if you're looking to implement big changes, you can take a more proactive approach by checking weekly or even daily. Setting the goals and objectives for your ideal spending plan can only take you so far; the actual execution is where the magic happens.

These tools will set you on the path to your destination—your money goals. You can't start any journey without first knowing where you are, nor can you change what you can't see. No more hiding from or avoiding your money. Dig deep and develop an awareness of your finances as the first step in working toward your goals and building your money muscle. Awareness starts with taking an inventory of what you have by creating your wealth snapshot (Chapter 7) and also knowing what you earn and spend by completing your budget. From there, you get to decide if any changes are needed as well as plan where you would like to go.

TAKING ACTION

Complete your past budget based on the steps outlined in the chapter to answer the questions:

> *How much money do you earn each month/year?*
> *How much money do you spend each month/year?*

(Feel free to think outside the box and use funky fonts and a colorful palette—to make it a masterpiece like Veronica did.)

Next, create your future budget—personalize it with your own title, and then get to planning how you would like to see your spending going forward (maybe you're inspired to spend less on glam by taking a do-it-yourself approach or plan to satisfy your fast-food cravings instead with air fryer fries). Whatever it is, write down your spending targets across the spending categories.

If the above is still a tad too overwhelming at this moment then here is an alternative to starting smaller but getting you into the budgeting mindset. Write down all your expenses for today, and if you fly through that then I challenge you to extend it slightly and write down all the expenses you had in the past week.

CHAPTER 9

INVESTING BUILDS WEALTH, BUT THIS DOESN'T HAVE TO BE SCARY

OKAY WE'VE WAITED LONG ENOUGH. If you're committed to building your money muscle then it's time we talk about investing. I get that the topic of investing might make your blood run cold and send your thoughts spiraling, especially if you're new to it. *What if I get it wrong? What if I lose everything?* But investing is also one of the surest ways to grow your wealth, so you'll have to learn about it to make money your thing. By the end of this chapter, I hope you agree that the benefits of investing are enticing enough to ditch those fear-based thoughts.

Let's start by breaking it down. Investing is a method to put your money to work with the expectation that it will grow in value. There are a variety of investment products that are available for you to purchase as an investor to accomplish this goal. I won't go into detail about the specific types of investments as that would take an entire book (or more) in itself, but what I do want to share is the purpose and power of investing. To illustrate why you should invest, it's helpful to compare investing to saving.

Let's say your goal is to have $1 million dollars. If you were to simply save your money in order to reach this goal, by putting away $1,000/month it would take you just over eighty-three years to get to that million. But I'm sure you also want to be alive and in good health to enjoy your million, so that won't do. If instead, you were to invest $1,000/month, and if your investments were to grow at a rate of 9% per year you would get to your million in just over twenty-three years. Yes, you saved yourself sixty years by investing! *And* in the savings example, you literally had to save up and put away 1 million dollars to achieve your goal, but in the investing example you saved $286,000 and the investing growth did the additional $714,000 for you. *Amazing!*

	Saving	Investing
Monthly Amount	$1,000	$1,000
Annual Rate of Return	0%	9%
Years to Reach $1,000,000	83	23
Your Contributions	$1,000,000	$286,000
Investment Growth	$0	$714,000

This is a great shortcut to wealth. Investing can save you years and loads of money on your journey to reach your goals. Unfortunately, what I see play out over and over again when I meet with women to talk about their money is they might have the saving part down pact but that's where it ends. And their savings are left sitting on the sidelines as cash in the bank.

Having the saving part down is great. But as I shared, socking it away as cash could mean that you don't reach your goals until age 100! But you deserve to have your money doing some of the heavy lifting too. In fact, this do-nothing approach could be harming your cash, as its value starts to erode due to inflation. You can think of inflation as the inevitable rise in prices year over year on the typical goods you purchase such as groceries and clothing. My mom used to always tell me that as a child she could buy a chocolate bar and a soda for a quarter. Sadly, that wouldn't even buy you a bite of a chocolate bar now. That's inflation in action.

The cost of living increases with inflation, and although it's a moving target, inflation has typically averaged around 2–3% per year. In times of extreme situations, like the world finds itself in post-Covid, inflation could even be much higher. If you allow your savings to sit idle without earning any kind of return, you can watch your stockpile of cash shrink like a balloon losing air over time. To maintain the purchasing power of your money, you need to grow it by at least the rate of inflation each year. And again, that is simply to preserve its value.

But you and your money are worthy of much more than simply keeping up with inflation. You put in so much time and energy into earning your money. Wouldn't it be nice for your money to also be working hard for you?

Investing is about putting your money to work so it can give back to you. The goal of investing is to maintain and even to grow your purchasing power (outpace inflation). The outcome of investing is different than simply saving. The intention of saving is all about preservation and paying for shorter-term goals and expenses. By investing, you're expecting a profit through growth and appreciation over time in the value of your investments.

Recently, I had a conversation with a client named Lucy. We'd been working together for several years at this point. When we first started, she completed the same budgeting exercise you began in Chapter 7 and discovered she was able to direct $500 per month toward her financial independence goal. We set up a contribution into her tax-deferred account each month, making it automatic so she would never miss a deposit.

Fast forward, and Lucy was still doing a fabulous job of growing her investments and, based on a pay raise, had been able to increase her monthly deposits to $750. When we initially set up the account, I created an investing plan for Lucy which we discussed at length. The plan took into consideration her risk preference and time frame to design the investment portfolio that would best suit her goals. Because she was young and had no intention of accessing this money until her retirement years, she was willing to take on some risk in her investments in return for a higher potential reward. Lucy had also been working on increasing her investing knowledge by attending my monthly lunch and learn sessions, which built her confidence around investing.

This was the perfect combination. We were able to discuss the investment options at length while I answered her questions and she was engaged throughout the process. Over the years, we continued to check in and made some allocation adjustments to the investments, and she continued to add to them monthly.

After six years of working together and investing, Lucy was in awe of the progress and growth of her accounts. She started from scratch.

And now she had over $60,000 in her retirement account. Seeing her efforts in action and her money working for her was a game changer. And what was even more exciting is that when we projected it outward based on her average return and monthly deposit, at that rate by age sixty she would have $1.3 million dollars. When Lucy heard this projection, the smile that spread across her face was contagious; she never imagined that she could become a millionaire on her own efforts (no lotto win required!).

It's client stories like Lucy's that help me hop out of bed in the morning, ready to help change lives and fortunes. By being a diligent saver combined with the power of investing, Lucy will be able to reach a level of wealth that she didn't dream was possible for her.

What's possible for Lucy is possible for you too. Open your mind to entertain even bigger money goals than you ever imagined for yourself.

I'm fortunate to get to see the power of investing firsthand for my clients. To know that the right combination of investing and patience really does work and can yield some pretty spectacular results. I can appreciate that this might be harder to put your faith in when you don't have that same front-row seat to wealth building that I have. But Lucy is a real person, seeing real results, and I want to make sure every woman out there has these same tools to help their money grow.

I love what I do and could go on all day sharing charts that illustrate the impact of investing. I can show you what it would look like if you put $100, $200, $300, $400, $500 (any dollar value) away each month and invested it. And I can demonstrate the growth potential at different potential rates of return.

Monthly Investment	Starting Age	Amount Deposited to Age 65 ($)	At 4% Annual ROR ($)	At 7% Annual ROR ($)	At 9% Annual ROR ($)
$100	25	48,000	118,196	262,481	468,132
	30	42,000	91,373	180,105	294,178
	40	30,000	51,413	81,007	112,112
	50	18,000	24,609	31,696	37,841
$200	25	96,000	236,392	524,963	936,264
	30	84,000	182,746	360,211	588,357
	40	60,000	102,826	162,014	224,224
	50	36,000	49,218	63,392	75,681
$300	25	144,000	354,588	787,444	1,404,396
	30	126,000	274,119	540,316	882,535
	40	90,000	154,239	243,022	336,337
	50	54,000	73,827	95,089	113,522
$400	25	192,000	472,785	1,049,925	1,872,528
	30	168,000	365,492	720,422	1,176,714
	40	120,000	205,652	324,029	448,449
	50	72,000	98,436	126,785	151,362
$500	25	240,000	590,981	1,312,407	2,340,660
	30	210,000	456,865	900,527	1,470,892
	40	150,000	257,065	405,036	560,561
	50	90,000	123,045	158,481	189,203

But instead of adding pages and pages to illustrate every possible scenario, I'll let you in on this secret. You'll always have more money if you can grow it by investing. I'm simplifying it here, and there are other factors at play. Investments can, and do, fluctuate in value. And there is of course risk, and potential for loss when it comes to investing as well. But over the long run, the stock markets have moved in an upward direction. Yes, there have been major market events that have had an impact on investment returns such as the financial crisis of 2007/2008 and more recently the global pandemic in 2020, but over the long term, the markets have always recuperated from these major events and continued their upward climb.

Now that you've seen a few examples of money growing as a result of investing, you might be wondering, but how is this all possible? Well, the major force at work when it comes to growing your money through investing is the power of compounding.

Let's talk a bit about compounding and how it works. When you put your money into an investment, the expectation is that it will increase in value. Depending on the investment product you use, this growth can come from appreciation in the price of the investment or from payments made by the investment. Keeping it simple, let's just say where it's coming from is irrelevant—but the main point is that it's growing and as it grows you leave it entirely invested. Or as it pays cash, that cash is also reinvested. As a result of leaving it, and not withdrawing the money, you're essentially allowing it all to continue to build upon itself. So compounding is essentially growth upon growth. Below is an example using numbers to illustrate this. In the chart, the investment is paying 5% interest each year, and then that interest is being reinvested (to also earn 5%):

Year	Value to Start the Year	Interest Paid	Total
1	$10,000	$500	$10,500
2	$10,500	$525	$11,025
3	$11,025	$551	$11,576

As you can see in the table, the interest being earned each year is increasing. And it isn't due to the return increasing as it has stayed at 5% per year in the example. It's due to the interest being paid on a larger starting balance each year, as the growth (interest paid) is being added to the principal and reinvested. The growth is happening *on* your growth.

Have you ever built a snowman? Don't worry if you live in a hot climate and prefer to avoid the white fluffy stuff, I can explain further. It all begins by collecting a small amount of snow by hand and then packing it into a snowball. Next, you get down on all fours and start rolling your ball in the snow. The fresh snow continues to cling to the growing ball, the circumference expanding exponentially. And before you know it that snowball has become so large that you have to call in your buddies to help push. Your freezing carrot nose sculpture comes to life by compounding in action.

And if this compounding concept is still a bit fuzzy, no problem. People often refer to it as "the magic of compounding," and really you aren't expected to know how magic works unless you are the magician performing the act. You can be the amazed observer of compounding and sit back and enjoy the show. The important part is participating in compounding by putting it into action for your money. No getting cold or rolling snow necessary.

Investing your money is how you can reap the benefits of compounding. But you may be wondering if investing is so magical, why do people still sit on the sidelines with their cash? And why isn't everyone investing?

A big piece of what stops people from investing is fear. This shows up in different phases of the investing process. There's the fear of the unknown if you've never invested before. And if you can manage to work past the initial scares, your fear may not completely subside. There are fears of losing money, of making the wrong investment decision, of missing out on an investment opportunity, and of buying or selling your investment at the wrong time. You'll have to face these monsters head-on if you want to reap the potential benefits of investing.

From my experience as a financial professional, the most common and impactful one that holds people back is the fear of getting started investing in the first place. Confession time, this is something I personally did. My very first exposure to the stock markets was in my seventh-grade computer class. We were learning how to use Microsoft Excel. My teacher assigned us a project of picking stocks and using Excel to track their prices to see how they performed over the next month. I was so excited because I loved money (still do). And although no real money was involved in the project, it gave me the thrill of possibly making millions in my fake portfolio, opening up the real possibility of making money later in my adult years.

This was the first time I'd ever heard of stocks. The teacher gave us a brief overview about how to look for companies that offered their shares for purchase on the stock exchange. He mentioned that those that were publicly traded and available for purchase would have a stock symbol.

That afternoon, when I got home from school, I sat on my bed brainstorming about how I might go about finding the best stocks to invest in. I didn't have any of the handy research tools at home then. The internet was still in its infancy and was a luxury we couldn't afford anyway. I had to get creative.

Scanning my bedroom, I realized the answer was right in front of me. I could choose the companies that made the stuff I loved and that I'd saved my hard-earned babysitting money to buy. If they were popular and a lot of people bought their stuff that had to mean that they were making lots of money. Right?

I decided to invest my fake money in my favorite products. I was just starting to wear makeup at the time, so I chose my favorite makeup brand for one. The clothes that I paid big dollars for were all made by Guess, so I picked that brand as well. And when I ran out of companies in my bedroom, I expanded my search through the rest of our house, even scanning the toothpaste tube to find out which company was providing our household essentials. After scouring my home, I had my list of companies ready.

The next day in class, I double-checked using the internet at school to verify that the companies I wanted to invest in were publicly traded. Then I found their stock symbols and entered them into my spreadsheet. I made my stock purchases, fully spending my fake $10,000, and I was ready to make some cash (and to beat Alex and Colin who sat on either side of me and were already bragging about how their picks would perform the best).

We had a few minutes at the start of each class that month to plot the progress of our portfolios. And although there were some ups and downs, overall I was thrilled to see mine increasing in value. When the thirty days were up we submitted our final results. The teacher posted the rankings for the top five performance on our portfolios the next day, and guess who made first place?

Me!

I was not an athletic person, and I had never had a moment where I won first place at anything, which made this victory even more amazing. I was an investing all-star!

My math mind was intrigued by this discovery of the stock

markets. The seed had been planted for my future career but it stayed dormant for many years. My next encounter with the stock markets was in my first year of college while taking an introduction to finance course. I had heard horror stories about the class, and the professor who had been teaching it for so long that he had taught parents of some of the current cohort. The rumors had me so scared that I lessened my course load in anticipation of the class.

Before the course even began, we were required to complete an entire textbook of lessons. I flipped through the pages and felt a surge of excitement. It was the same thrill I had as a child when I got to do my sister's math homework. It was comfortable and familiar. I blew through the lessons, enjoying every page.

From my winning stock picking in seventh grade to my love for a finance course that nobody else found joy in, you might be thinking that investing came easy and naturally for me. That I was born to invest. And you might assume that these experiences probably led me to get a very early start to investing my own money.

But nope.

Several of my close friends in business school were taking what they were learning and actively investing their cash from student loans or from their part-time gigs. But not me, no way. The stock market felt like an inaccessible secret club. One that was strictly reserved for people with lots of money who were experts at investing. A bunch of old rich guys gathered around a bulky boardroom table talking stocks, where I clearly didn't belong. I still carried the baggage of growing up poor, assuming people like me weren't meant to invest. Despite my early experience practicing and my growing finance knowledge, I wasn't confident enough to be investing. It took me some time to get started.

In fact, I didn't begin until I was working with a financial advisor, years after completing my degree. It literally took me working in a business whose primary objective is to invest people's money for me to be comfortable enough to begin. By that time I had already lost out on a good five years of compounding growth. Had I skipped some trips to the bar and managed to save $200 per month from age nineteen to twenty-four, even if I saved nothing beyond those five years and just let it grow and compound, I would have had about $600,000[2] at age sixty-five. Those five years cost me over half a million dollars.

I practiced investing at the age of twelve. I received formal post-secondary education on advanced concepts of investing. And *still*, I was afraid and lacked the confidence to invest. So this is me saying to you with complete empathy and understanding—if you're hesitant, if you have fears around investing, I get it.

I really, *really* get it.

Fears about investing are powerful. They're an enormously large barricade standing between you and the power of compounding. The fear can come from money messages picked up in your youth, insecurities about your financial literacy, perceived mistakes or bad decisions you've made in the past, or just not feeling like you fit into the old boys club. But if you're fully on board to make money your thing, you must push past your fears. You'll have to invest.

But here's the good news: it doesn't have to be scary.

Investing is an integral part of growing your money and building wealth. And that should fill you with happy thoughts. If fear has been holding you back from investing, let's kick it to the curb. You deserve

2   Compounded at 9% annual rate of return.

to reap the rewards of investing and to enjoy watching your money grow. Here are some ways that you can make investing less scary.

Ditch the High Interest Debt before You Invest

When it comes to investing, the sooner you can start the better. But if you're carrying a balance on your credit card(s), then investing should come after you've paid that off first. The type of debt I'm referring to here is that which holds a high interest rate. Or what we investment professionals also refer to as bad debt. High can vary depending on the type of debt but I would generally associate it with double-digit interest—so let's say over 10%. If you have a credit card that carries a high-interest rate but you pay it off in full each month that's great and can assist in building your credit score. What I'm specifically referring to here is when you splurge on the designer bag opting to pay for it . . . eventually. And then proceed to pay 18% interest while the unpaid balance sits on your card. And although compound interest is a wonderful phenomenon when it's working for you, the opposite is true when it's working against you. Compound interest on debt can add months or even years to paying off your purchases. And with the amount of interest you end up paying you could have bought two more fancy purses!

How can paying off high-interest debt first make investing less scary—you might be wondering. If you carry this bad debt while also investing you have to beat your credit card interest to make it worth it. That means you may have to earn 20% or more on your investments to justify investing instead of paying down your 18–19% credit card. That's a big rate of return to aim for on your investments when the annual average return for being invested in the US stock markets has been about 9–10%. And although in a really good year in the markets that could be feasible, it's not something consistently achievable. Investing gurus don't even claim to be able to get those 20%+ types of returns consistently on a yearly basis. To make this possible you would have to be an investing genius and likely need to take some big gambles on some high-risk investments. Which would definitely make investing scary. Taking undue risk in the markets to shoot for ultra-high returns is a stressful strategy and cause for sleepless nights. Paying off the high-interest debt first can help to avoid any return performance pressure and unrealistic expectations.

Practice with a Fake Portfolio

We've all heard the phrase "practice makes perfect"; well, this translates to investing as well. If you don't have much experience investing or if you're looking to invest for the first time, then why not get some practice first?

This is a great way to ease into it. Like I did for my seventh-grade computer assignment, you can use fake money. Try creating a mock portfolio, which is essentially a fake stock portfolio. You can use a spreadsheet as I did to record all your picks, or most stock apps or online brokerages will also offer the practice portfolio feature.

Getting practice investing will build your confidence around making investment decisions in a safe environment. There's no real money to lose, and only experience to gain.

And if you have teens in your life, this is a great way to introduce them to investing. A woman attending my Investing 101 course shared she did this with her daughter at the age of fifteen—had her invest a fake $2,500 portfolio and track how it performed. And she very generously upped the ante by saying whatever value her daughter could get the portfolio to at the age of eighteen she would gift her that in real dollars toward her first car purchase. Well, turns out her daughter might be the next Warren Buffett as she built her fake account up to $7,000 over three years!

Using a mock portfolio to simulate what you would do with real money is a fabulous exercise to learn from. One of the most important elements to investing is self-discipline, which can be hard to maintain when the stock markets are behaving more like your favorite roller coaster at Six Flags. Using a fake portfolio is a great way to see how you might react in response to big market moves. And a good way to gauge your comfort level with risk. Maybe you assumed you would be cool as a cucumber if your investments were to go down 10%, but when you see it actually occur you find yourself wanting to flee for the exit. It's also a great way to check in with some of the emotions that might come up when you invest and to see if those are getting the best of you, and influencing your decisions. If so, this isn't a time to judge, but more so to get a better sense of self-awareness around investing. It may mean you need some more time to get comfortable and practice. Or that maybe you would prefer some assistance, which of course is also an option. There are a variety of supports from robo-advisors, to financial professionals that are available to guide you and help you through the investment decision-making process.

Set aside Some Savings

If you're investing money that you may need to access tomorrow or next week if an unplanned expense were to arise, well then investing is going to be a very stressful experience. The markets move up and

the markets move down. You never want to be caught in a position of needing quick access to your cash when markets are down
substantially, which would require you to sell at a loss. The way to
avoid this and to make investing less scary would be to have a nice
cushion of cash that you can easily access. This way you don't have
to be monitoring your investments like a hawk when your car starts
acting up again and making that strange clicking sound. Having a
surplus account provides the peace of mind that you can make that
appointment with the mechanic rather than holding your breath
each time you go for a drive, fingers crossed that you make it to your
destination. With an emergency surplus ready and available, you
can accept the ups and downs of investing as it won't have a major
impact on your short-term cash needs. I will go into the details about
creating your surplus fund in Chapter 11, but for now, I will say this:
before you start investing have your emergency/rainy day account
already in place or be actively working to build it. This will relieve
some of the pressure that the shorter-term fluctuations of the stock
markets can bring.

Ditch the Peer Pressure

I highly encourage conversations about money. So by all means bring
it up in chats with colleagues, friends, family, and ask questions and
get input from those you trust. But a bit of a disclaimer that goes
along with this is to be careful when the topic of conversation centers on *investing*. Take what you hear with a grain of salt. And know
that you may not always be getting the full picture. I'm not accusing
these people in your life of being liars. But, generally, folks like to
boast about their big wins yet aren't willing to give up any details on

the duds. And there's nothing wrong with this. Who wants to talk about losing money?

A story about watching your investment flop 90% doesn't carry the same punch as the big 200% return on a clever stock pick. Know you're likely only getting a tiny glimpse, not the full story. If someone is eager to talk about a stock they purchased that went up 75% in a matter of months, remember it's one investment in their entire portfolio. If they have others that have gone down, stayed flat, or didn't move up as much, then this doesn't translate to their overall return being 75%, although your mind might play tricks on you and want to jump to that conclusion.

Try not to get caught up in the envy of investment FOMO. Remember you're likely only getting a sneak peek of the good stuff. And you cannot recreate what others are doing based on this partial information. It's valuable to learn from others, but don't simply try to replicate them or you might find yourself chasing unreal and impossible goals and never being happy with what you have.

Become Clear about Your Intentions

Are you investing or are you gambling? Get clear on your goals when it comes to investing and what you're looking to accomplish. This adds to the previous point about peer pressure—if you're following hot stock tips with an aim to "win big" your intentions might be leaning toward gambling more than investing.

If you throw your money into an investment simply from hearsay, hoping to win big, that sounds more like taking a gamble than investing. And if that's the case it's important to acknowledge you're gambling and set some strict limits on what you're willing to wager or bet.

With gambling, you have to be comfortable with losing it all.

If you're *not* comfortable with potentially losing it all, then it sounds like you're looking to invest. Choose wisely. Set investment criteria.

Investing is a longer-term approach to building wealth. It might include doing research and gathering information so you can justify the decision. Warren Buffett, the guru of investing, spends countless hours reading research reports and analyzing companies before he is willing to invest. And although I'm not suggesting you give up your social life to spend your Friday nights scrutinizing the quarterly financials of publicly traded companies. It does give some context to how investment decisions should be given some time and consideration. You might do this due diligence directly, or rely on the support of a financial professional.

Approaching it from an investment perspective, rather than gambling, is like getting to be one of the sharks on *Shark Tank*, the show where rich entrepreneurs decide if they are willing to make an investment in a business idea. Do the sharks give their money to anyone that steps into the tank? Nope. It takes a lot to convince them to invest. And they aren't exactly strapped for cash, but they are still extremely picky about who or what they are willing to invest their hard dollars in. One can only assume they got to be as successful as they are by having meticulous standards for their investment decisions. The sharks are careful about who they give money to because they want some assurance that they will be paid back on their investment. When your intention is investing, treat your money the same way a shark does. This is your hard-earned cash so it's okay to be picky about where it goes.

When your intentions are clear, investing is far less scary. If you're willing to take a gamble, then you must also accept the possibility of losing everything. Don't gamble what you cannot afford to lose. You wouldn't take your entire retirement savings to Vegas and risk your financial independence by placing it *all* on red. Investing isn't the same as gambling. The intention of investing is for longer-term growth. You can and should be diligent and discerning with who and what gets your money.

Know Your Time Horizon

Getting clear on your time frame and investing accordingly is one of the best things you can do for your money. By time horizon, I'm referring to when you need the money for its specific purpose. You likely have a few separate time horizons for each of your goals. Here's an example from Nicole, a fabulous client and woman who is happily making *money her thing*. Nicole is a single parent and has a goal to fund her daughter's college because she really wished she had had support for her education when she was pulling double shifts at the local pub to afford tuition. Her daughter is only ten years old now, so that leaves Nicole with about eight more years to work on that goal.

Secondly, she's saving for her financial freedom. Nicole is super passionate about the work she does now as a life coach so is unsure when she will retire. But she would like to be financially secure and have the freedom and flexibility to do so by the age of sixty. Nicole is currently thirty-five years old, which makes her financial freedom horizon twenty-five years.

The information about her time horizon for each of these goals gives valuable insight into creating Nicole's investing plan. Time horizon classifications vary, but I usually break them down as follows: 0–3 years short term, 4–10 years medium term, and 10 years plus long term. Thus, Nicole has a medium-term goal with her daughter's education and a longer-term goal for her financial freedom.

Investing for your time frame is like dressing appropriately for the weather. When you walk out of your house wearing a parka in a snowstorm it means you're well prepared. The same goes for investing. For longer-term goals, you can take on some more risk in your investments especially if you don't plan on touching the money for decades, like Nicole. Here, you're always dressed for the weather. And for shorter-term goals, you likely want to stay more conservatively positioned to limit the volatility. You don't want to invest too risky for shorter-term goals, nor too conservatively for longer-term goals. Getting specific on your time frames and letting that inform the investment piece, rather than simply hoping the money is there when you need it, can alleviate some of the uncertainty that comes with investing.

Be Sure to Diversify

Being diversified is another way to make investing less scary. As the saying goes, don't put all your eggs in one basket. Think of diversifying like planning the snack spread for your kid's birthday party. A variety of chip flavors, a fruit and veggie tray, ice cream cake, dairy-free cupcakes, gluten-free brownies, vegan cookies, and making sure *everything* is peanut free, should leave no child left unfed. Diversifying among your investments doesn't guarantee against loss but it does help to minimize risk and reduce some volatility. If you were to invest in only two different stocks and then tomorrow news breaks that the one company in your portfolio is filing for bankruptcy—well, the value of your account would likely move . . . by a lot. And that would be scary.

But if your investments are allocated among twenty-five stocks, then that same scenario would have far less of an impact. You can diversify your portfolio by country, type of investment (i.e., stock versus bond), number of investments, and industry to name a few. There are also many different investment products that hold a variety of stocks within the investment itself, so diversification can also be easily achieved by using this type of tool.

Diversification is an ongoing diligent strategy to be mindful of when it comes to investing. And when implemented, it can help ensure that you don't need a bottle of wine on hand each time you view your account.

Investing is a wonderful way to get your money working for you and to give your savings a boost. And the ideas listed above offer ways to reduce some of the fear you may have about investing. Being afraid can leave you sitting on the sidelines and missing out on the gift of compounding. I don't want that for you, and I hope now that you're reading this you don't either! So, if you haven't started investing yet, the time to start is *now*. Whatever you do, don't wait! The fears might try to sneak in—but don't let them; you are making money your thing! And let me share one more compounding example to show why you cannot keep putting this off.

One of the biggest contributors to the power of compounding is time. And I can explain this with a scenario between two women who started investing but with one getting a head start. Michelle and Jessica are the same age. But Michelle got an early start to investing at the age of nineteen (the age I wish I would have started because it could've had me over half a million bucks richer in retirement). Michelle calculated she could realistically save $2,000/year, so to accomplish this she began investing $167/month. She then stopped

investing at age twenty-seven but didn't touch the money and let it
continue to grow and compound. Her friend Jessica realized the value
of investing a bit later on and she got started at age twenty-seven
(just when Michelle had stopped making additional deposits), also
putting away $167/month or $2,000/year. But Jessica saved much
longer as she continued to do this until she was sixty-five years old.
For this example, I've used an average rate of return of 10% per year
on their investments over the duration. Now the question is, at age
sixty-five who has more money? Michelle who started earlier but only
added to her investments for eight years or Jessica who started later
but continued to make deposits to her investments for thirty-nine
years?

	Michelle	Jessica
Total Amount Invested	$16,000	$78,000
Number of Years Depositing	8	39
Compounded Growth Portion	$1,019,161	$805,185
Value of Investment at Age 65	$1,035,161	$883,185

And the answer is: *Michelle!*

Michelle only put away $16,000 which is $62,000 less than Jessica
and she *still* had more money at sixty-five. This illustrates how important time is as a factor of compounding. It might be hard to get your
head around how this is mathematically possible, but the point of
the example is the earlier you start the better! If you're not nineteen
years old like Michelle that doesn't mean it's too late and all hope is
lost; I didn't start at nineteen either. Whatever age you are, the point
of this example is that you're better to start today than a year or two
from now. So no more excuses and no more holding back. No matter

what stage of life you're in, the sooner you can begin the better. Invest right now and embrace the power of compounding!

TAKING ACTION

Practice investing as I did in grade 7. Pretend I've given you $10,000 to invest in your own stock portfolio. Pick the companies you'd like to invest in. Type "stock symbol for (company name)" on an internet search to get the symbol if you don't know it. Once you have that, use a stock app or search the web for what price the stock is currently trading at. This will provide you with the current price per share, and then use that information to decide how many shares you'll purchase (don't forget about your $10,000 budget).

Using a spreadsheet or any method of tracking that works for you, log the amount of shares you bought and the price you purchased them at with your fake money. And then peak in on how your stock picks are doing every so often by checking on the price. The US and Canadian stock markets are open Monday–Friday 9:30 a.m.-4 p.m. EST so the prices will continue to fluctuate during those hours.

If you aren't ready to take on this homework assignment yet then try starting small. Dip your toes in the investing waters by downloading a stock tracker app on your phone. Maybe enter a few stocks for companies you know well and purchase from. When I explained the stock picking assignment to Ivy her top picks were Apple (loves her iPad) and of course our fav fast-food spot McDonald's!

PART 3

MAKING YOUR MONEY CONFIDENCE UNSHAKEABLE

CHAPTER 10

PAY ATTENTION. NOBODY WILL CARE ABOUT YOUR MONEY AS MUCH AS YOU DO

NOW THAT YOU'VE DONE the work on building your money muscle; you don't want to give back or lose any of your hard-earned confidence. It's time to solidify your money confidence and make it unshakeable. Staying engaged with your money is so important when you're making money your thing. Because at the end of the day, it's your money and the person who will love and care about it the most will always be you.

This means you must pay attention. You need to be an active participant in discussions and decisions being made about *your* money. Don't give up control entirely and fully outsource this important responsibility to someone else. Choosing to remain in the dark about your finances is not how you go about making money your thing.

Too often, I see women hand over all financial decision-making to someone else who they have decided would be better equipped to handle it, whether it be a spouse, friend or family member, or even a financial professional. But you belong in that equation. You know what you need. *You* are the best person to represent your money.

Nothing in life is certain. You could separate from your partner or spouse, the financially savvy family member might get too busy to continue to help you, or your financial professional may retire or leave the business. If you're fully relying on another person to take the lead on your money, their absence could rock your wealth.

And what happens if the person you've given control to doesn't act with your best interests in mind? It's devastating to see people suffer financial losses at the hands of someone else because they gave up control. But sadly this can happen if you aren't paying attention.

I encountered a couple who lost their life savings after entrusting a friend with their finances. And I work with several divorced women who have had to rebuild from scratch after leaving the financial decisions to their spouses, only to find out that their husbands weren't the money experts they claimed to be. It's scary, I know. And in no way do I want you to feel completely paranoid and paralyzed by fear.

I share these stories because these situations don't have to happen. There are things you can do to protect yourself from financial losses. Staying involved when it comes to your money offers an extra level of surveillance to ensure your best interests remain at the forefront.

Being engaged means never fully giving up control or deferring entirely to others when it comes to your money. That includes giving up full control to a partner or spouse.

A client named Olivia decided it was best to have her husband Andrew fully manage the household finances during their marriage because of his accounting background. Olivia kept busy raising their two children and figured Andrew was better suited to managing the money. Finances seemed to be abundant for the family of four and Olivia enjoyed the flexibility and freedom it brought.

But after a twenty-year marriage, she was blindsided when Andrew left her for another woman. When he immediately started working with a lawyer to start the divorce proceeding, Olivia followed suit and hired one as well. Her lawyer was seeking ongoing alimony support for the next several years, since she had been out of the workforce raising their children, along with the equal division of their assets.

Sadly, there was more bad news to come for Olivia. While trying to account for all the assets that would be considered in the matrimonial division, her lawyer couldn't find any money.

Based on Andrew's salary over the past two decades (combined with hers during her working years) the numbers didn't add up. There were no assets or money to show for their years of working. The home had minimal equity in it and the savings and investments didn't amount to much.

Her lawyer analyzed the documents from all the separate investment accounts and discovered that Olivia's ex had been treating the stock markets like a casino. He'd gambled most of their life savings away on poor investments.

Listening to her share this story in my office made my chest tight. I gripped my pen so hard I thought it would snap. I never thought I would encounter someone firsthand who had gone through such a dramatic series of events.

I predicted the ending scene before the words had come out of Olivia's mouth. I knew that when it comes to splitting assets you can't get something out of nothing. And that's exactly what had happened to her. Despite assuming that the finances were well taken care of and that they were in a healthy position, in actuality she would have to restart from scratch.

Olivia had trusted Andrew fully to take the lead in their financial life. He was the obvious choice for the job as the numbers guy. She had no reason to doubt his capabilities or suspect he would make such poor investment decisions.

I strive to keep the focus inspiring and empowering when it comes to money stories. And no, this story was *not* a positive money experience to read about. But sharing Olivia's story is important because giving up control to a spouse is the most common form of disengaging with one's finances. Olivia's experience is unfortunately one of several financially shattering situations I've encountered when a woman has allowed her spouse to completely take over all financial matters.

If her story has you thinking you would be better off outsourcing to a third party, such as a financial professional, know that there are risks to fully giving up control in those instances as well. I'm sure you've heard nightmare news stories of Ponzi schemes and other unsavory characters having taken advantage of their clients. Stories like that are extremely hard to hear, I know. But it serves as an important reminder that there are risks to fully giving up control to anyone, and that also includes professionals.

I want to assure you that there's a lot that goes on behind the scenes to protect investors. Investment regulatory bodies are constantly improving surveillance measures and stricter compliance practices are being implemented in the industry. But some bad apples have managed to get into the industry and engage in unethical or illegal practices.

My goal in sharing these stories is not to make you paranoid and feel that all hope is lost in being able to trust others. What I want to do is bring awareness to why it's *so* important to pay attention and stay engaged when it comes to your money. And I want to stress here that the risk lies in *fully* giving up control of your finances. As in completely passing off to someone else, with no further participation, communication, or check-ins. The risk is greatly reduced if you're able to stay engaged and involved in some capacity.

If you or someone you know has said, "My partner/spouse handles our money" or, "My advisor looks after my finances," it's time for a change. As you now see there are dangers to fully giving up control of your money to anyone. In a relationship, it's essential to talk about finances with your partner and be involved in the money decisions. And if you enlist the assistance of a financial professional, you can stay in the know through regular check-ins and open communication.

If you can take away the powerful lesson that fully giving up control of your finances is not in your best interest, then at the very least these devastating money stories can save others.

And if you're wondering what followed for Olivia—fortunately, her experience didn't leave her completely jaded and unwilling to trust again. She's engaged in the process and planning for her big financial goals.

This is a major mindset shift if you've been taking a hands-off approach with your money. But participation is required if you're ready to make money your thing. Don't get me wrong; dividing and conquering in a relationship or outsourcing to a professional are efficient strategies for managing the competing priorities of life. But when it comes to your hard-earned cash, you don't want to ever fully step away from that responsibility. It's your money at the end of the day, so you get the starring role.

I recently had a conversation with a woman named Francis, who is eighty-two years old, about her finances. Her husband had passed away several months prior and her friend suggested she talk to me, knowing that I am passionate about supporting women investors. Francis shared that stock picking was a hobby of her husband. She recalled watching him slouched over the newspaper each morning deep in thought reading through the stock quotes that were only accessible as day-old information at the time. Francis never really understood why he enjoyed it as much as he did. She found it redundant and boring.

But seeing how passionate and dedicated he was to it, Francis decided that she should probably learn more about it. It was after all her money, too. One morning she asked him to explain it to her. He looked up surprised by her request but quickly pulled over a chair eager to talk stocks. Over the years, he taught her everything he knew and loved about investing. Francis listened intently and learned. Candidly, she disclosed that she never shared the same level of passion or excitement that her husband had for stock picking, but she did come to understand it. As her knowledge grew over the years, she also became an active participant in which stocks they bought. She challenged her husband on certain picks and brought her own investment ideas to the table. They were an investing duo. And with great rates of return over the years, they were quite the dream team.

And they continued to be, right up until his passing.

On our call, Francis shared what stocks she'd bought and sold over the months since his passing. And we talked about the markets and what she was eyeing as potential opportunities.

I was in awe.

I can say that Francis was the first woman in her eighties that I've ever talked stocks with like that. She had it down.

She knew her stuff and I loved every minute of our conversation.

The best part was when I called her an anomaly and told her how inspired I was by her. She responded she was flattered and had never really thought of it that way. She just knew it was important to have an understanding about what was going on with her money.

Yessss! Francis! Money was her thing!

By the end of our call, I knew Francis had the investment stuff under control. I loved talking to her and told her I would be honored to work with her if she was ever looking for a partner. But I assured her that, ultimately, she was doing all the right things and those years spent being an active participant had served her well.

Francis is an inspiration. She was part of a generation where the vast majority left investing and financial decision-making up to their husbands. But not Francis. Even though she wasn't all that interested, she still opted to learn and be an active participant. So much so that she was still a stock market wizard into her eighties.

If you're ready to embrace your own inner Francis (because I know if you're reading this book you have the makings of a money master too) one of the best ways you can stay engaged and show up to represent your financial needs is through advocating for your money. Stand up for what's *yours*; nobody else will love it as much as you do.

* * *

At a recent "lunch and learn" presentation I hosted at my office someone asked, "What do you mean by advocating for your money?"

It's a fabulous question and something I want to explain further here. And I'm going to do so with a non-money-related example, by sharing a story about my daughter because she's my little boss lady.

One afternoon, after picking Ivy up from school she demanded, "I want McDonald's." (She can be a tad feisty after putting in a full day of learning.)

I used the typical parent trying to teach manners response by asking, "Aren't you forgetting something?"

"Pleaseeeeeeeeeeee." She corrected.

"Okay, fine," I said. And this had nothing to do with rewarding her for being less demanding. It's just that I share my daughter's love for McDonald's, so it's not hard to convince me. McDonald's it was! At the restaurant when we got to the front of the line, I leaned over to ask Ivy what she wanted, since her preferences were a moving target most days and I couldn't seem to keep up with her changing tastes.

"Fries," she said.

And then followed up with "please" when she saw the unimpressed look on my face. As I stood back up and leaned in to place the order Ivy exclaimed, "Oh wait." She tugged at my sleeve to pull me down and in for a whisper.

"Actually I want *fresh* fries," she corrected.

"I'm not asking for that," I whispered back, embarrassed that she was treating McDonald's like a Michelin-star restaurant but also sort of intrigued about whether that was even a feasible request. "You order it then," I suggested.

We came out from our huddle and Ivy moved in front of me to stand closer to the till with her head held high. "I want fresh fries, please."

"Okay." The cashier said as she rang in Ivy's special order.

I don't know if I was more shocked that apparently being polite was easy to remember with strangers, or that this woman seemed completely unfazed by Ivy's high-maintenance request. It was all quite odd.

We stood to the side, having to wait longer for Ivy's steaming hot fries to exit the deep fryer.

When our order was ready, I followed Ivy with the tray to a booth in the corner. I couldn't resist reaching over to grab one of the highly anticipated piping hot fries. And all I can say is that I didn't think it was possible, but my love for McDonald's grew when I got a taste of Ivy's *fresh* fries.

Anyone who knows me can attest I'm a fry addict, but on that day, Ivy upped the ante. It changed the way I order fries forever (I highly recommend it).

That day, my daughter gave me an excellent example of the meaning of advocating for yourself. Ivy knew what she wanted and exactly how she wanted it. And she wasn't embarrassed, afraid, or apologetic about asking for that. She was confident and polite, but she didn't back down from speaking her mind and being true to her wants and needs. And the result was delicious!

That, my friends, is self-advocacy at work.

And if my six-year-old daughter can do it, you can do it too.

Self-advocacy is important in all aspects of your life, and this is especially true when it comes to your money. And Amanda is my favorite example of advocating for your money.

Amanda reached out to me initially over the phone on a Friday afternoon which I remember vividly because I was at a kids' play place with my daughter and her cousin. I answered the call, forgetting that I had forwarded my work phone. Normally I wouldn't attempt a work call from a location full of screaming children. It doesn't give the best first impression.

I planned to interject right away and suggest we connect at a better time, but there was a directness and authority that radiated from her. And I was captivated to follow her lead right from the start.

I booked it to a far corner of the building, hoping to find a quiet spot as Amanda introduced herself and got straight to the point. She shared that she'd been working with an advisor for the last few years but wasn't satisfied. Actively looking to make a change, she was interviewing advisors and wanted to include me in her shortlist.

We set a time to meet, which I committed to memory, having no place to take notes in my position huddled next to a trampoline. I was excited to meet her in person. I love working with strong, empowered women.

When our meeting time arrived the following week, she didn't disappoint. She was dressed in a smart business suit with a large bold red necklace and had a pile of papers neatly stacked in front of her. I felt a tad underprepared with only my notebook, a pen and wearing absolutely no accessories.

We shook hands and then it was straight to business. She referenced the page in front of her and started with a question. After I had the opportunity to respond, she looked back down at her paper again and then asked me another. That's when I realized her page was full of questions for me. Many, *many* questions.

This really was an interview and I was being grilled.

I loved it.

In front of me sat a woman who knew exactly what she wanted and she wouldn't settle for any less.

She'd done her research and come up with wonderful questions. She was advocating for her money and I was confident that whether she chose to work with me or someone else, she would find the right fit for her.

Amanda reinvigorated my pride in being a woman. She was empowered and not willing to sacrifice or tiptoe around the important topic of her money. She was honoring herself by staying true to her needs and not lowering her standards. And in that meeting, I imagined my little fresh French Fry monster growing up to continue being bold and advocating for herself like Amanda, which gave me the warm fuzzies.

We can all use some of Amanda's advocacy. Women too often forget that they have every right to stand up and vocalize what they want and need. And if you aren't used to doing it, it can be uncomfortable and intimidating. But you'll always be the best person to represent your needs, nobody can read your mind, and if you don't do it, you might get stuck eating the cold soggy fries.

Your money is your money, and that means that you'll always be the one who cares about it the most. It's your job, your duty, to do what is right for your money. And no, it's not bossy or high-maintenance. If for some reason it still feels a tad unfamiliar for you, throw in a "please" or "thank you" if that helps, or find another method that works for you. But never lose sight of the importance of being the number one advocate for your money.

You saw the importance of being an engaged and active participant with your money earlier in this chapter. And further to that you also need to stand up for what is right for your financial life. Below I offer a few ideas on how you can settle into the role of advocate for your money.

Create Your List of Non Negotiables

Take the time to get clear on your money expectations. And it helps to write them down. You aren't a passive observer in your money story; you are the main character! You get to create the storyline. So at this moment, I'm asking you to truly think about exactly what is it that you want? Take your time and be honest with yourself and come from a place of possibilities (as discussed in Chapter 3). Close your eyes and imagine exactly where you see yourself in 5, 10, 20, 30+ years—where do you want to be with your finances and what does it feel like? Get specific, such as—working with a professional to complete a financial plan, becoming debt free in three years, buying a dream vacation property to enjoy with your family in seven years, saving enough to be free to retire whenever you choose. Advocating all starts by getting crystal clear on exactly what you want.

Find out What You Don't Know

We've all heard the phrase "you don't know what you don't know." Don't let this willful blindness cloud your financial life. Do your research, ask questions, and even question yourself. Taking the time to learn more when it comes to your money will have you feeling better equipped to ask the right questions. Read financial articles, listen to a podcast, or ask a friend. Opening your mind to a variety of resources will help you to uncover concepts and ideas that you might never have encountered before. These new ideas can help you think outside of the box, and learn what's possible when it comes to your money expectations. Have you been simply accepting things as is because you didn't know there were any other options? I had no idea that requesting *fresh* fries was an option, but Ivy opened my eyes to the possibilities by simply asking the question. And now I'm a fast-food restaurant's nightmare.

Stay Engaged at All Times

I've shared the dangers of fully giving up control when it comes to your money in this chapter. Don't pass off responsibility for your money to someone else. Show up to advocate and be a loving representative of your money. Working with your spouse or a financial professional is still a great option—but the key is working *together* and staying involved. Think of it as a partnership, and you are always in the know. Staying involved ensures your best interests are always at the forefront because you'll always be the person who knows *you* best.

Interview for the Job

If you choose to work with a professional to assist you on your wealth goals, commit to finding the right fit. Like Amanda, treat the search process as an interview. You choose who is hired to fill this very important position, not the other way around. And just like you're in control of who is hired for the job, if the person isn't meeting your expectations you also get to make the firing decisions too. Take time to create your list of interview questions. And if you want a hand, below are some ideas for questions to ask:

- Are you taking on new clients?
- Is there a minimum on how much someone would need to have as investible assets to work with you?

- What is your education background and experience level in this role? (If they have a whole array of designations and letters after their name go ahead and ask what they mean.)
- Do you provide financial planning? Is it done at an extra cost?
- What is your investment philosophy? What type of investments do you use? Can I be involved in the investment selection?
- What service level can I expect? What would be the frequency of review meetings or calls?
- What is the cost or fees for working together? Are there additional costs that I should be aware of?

Own It

Be prepared to be brave. It might not feel comfortable stepping into this role of money advocate especially if you've taken more of a passive role up until now. But you're looking out for what is best for you and putting your needs first, and there's nothing wrong with that. You deserve it and your money does too. Hold your head up high and move forward with confidence because nobody puts *you* in the corner.

You know you best, so stay engaged and in the know, when it comes to *your* money. Nobody will love your hard-earned cash as much as you do. Be the spokesperson—asking for what you want or need and not backing down. You deserve to have the freshest of fresh fries.

TAKING ACTION

When it comes to your money which parts do you know about, and which are you in the dark about? Go find out about it!

Examples:

- What is the interest rate on your credit card?
- What is the balance left on your mortgage?
- Who is the beneficiary on your retirement savings account?
- If you work with a financial professional what is the cost/fee you're paying for their services?

Start with a few but aim to get to know 100% because that's where the unshakeable confidence takes hold.

CHAPTER 11

KEEPING THE FOCUS ON WHAT YOU CAN CONTROL

IN THE LAST CHAPTER we talked about staying in the know when it comes to your money. But there will be elements that you can't fully know the outcome for, even if you've built your money muscle and are advocating for your cash.

While you're mastering making money your thing, accept that you'll encounter obstacles on your journey. Unplanned life events can happen anytime, making it all feel very unpredictable at times. What if you . . .

- Lose your job
- Get divorced
- Have a health challenge
- Get hit with a major unplanned expense
- Find your investments are impacted by a recession
- Run out of money in retirement years

The unknowns of life, coupled with the movement of the financial markets, can impact your money significantly. Unfortunately, neither you nor I possess psychic money abilities, and so these are factors we can't account for until they actually happen. Acceptance of what you cannot control is key when it comes to your money. And there's a lot that's out of your control as it relates to money which may have you feeling like a top spinning aimlessly.

The good news, on the flipside, is there's also a lot you *can* do for your money. Staying focused on what you can control is a much better use of your energy.

This was exactly the strategy that I used with a client named Rachel who started working with me years ago when she was in the midst of a stressful divorce. At the mercy of the endless back and forth through lawyers, she tried her hardest to keep a brave face for her two daughters. Much of what she was going through felt completely out of her control. The legal system suggested how the assets should be divided, including the family home, all the bank accounts, and the investment accounts. And her ex was extremely difficult to communicate with—he fired a few lawyers through the process, so even the hope for a speedy divorce was outside her control. The full process took years and left Rachel exhausted.

On top of the extreme stress of the whole experience, Rachel was thrown abruptly into the driver's seat of managing her finances. It was all completely new to her as her ex had taken charge of the finances during their marriage. She confessed at our first meeting that she had never even had her own bank account.

There was a lot going on in Rachel's financial life, and it would've been easy for her to throw her hands up, giving in to defeat. She could've caved from the complete lack of control and frustration she felt. But Rachel was a fighter and was not ready to concede just yet and that was what brought her to meet with me.

I took vigorous notes at our meeting, following the twists and turns of her story to get a clear picture of where she stood. Her divorce had thrown her off course. She was no longer on the same financial path she had in mind while she was married. *But* she was starting a new journey, one that she would be able to design, which was also exciting. There were a lot of moving parts, but I assured her that we would take it one step at a time.

No more letting her financial life happen *to* her; I was about to guide her toward taking charge. We focused on her needs and goals and what *was* in her control to make it a reality.

Over the following months she was able to accomplish the following:

- Creating a new wealth snapshot so she had an inventory of where she now stood with her finances
- Designing her "Master Money Plan" (what she chose to call her forward looking budget) for tracking and allocating her monthly income and expenses—where she wanted to be seeing her money go
- Planning for her new independent financial dreams—including her desire to continue her charitable efforts and hit her ten-year target of raising $100k for a cause that meant a lot to her
- Having a super savings strategy to add to her longer-term investments for her financial freedom goal
- Celebrating her financial independence achievements with a trip to Mexico with her daughters (guilt-free because it aligned with her goal to have new experiences with her girls)

Rachel went through a major unplanned life transition. But she never gave up or gave in to what was happening to her. Instead she focused on what she *could* do. The change I see in Rachel from where she is now compared to our very first meeting is remarkable. Her entire demeanor shifted and she stands taller, with the confidence she exudes. Rachel is empowered, and she's creating the financial life of her dreams.

In a world full of uncertainty it's important to acknowledge that there will always be factors that are out of your control when it comes to your money. As I write, we've recently experienced a global pandemic that reminded us all just how much is out of our control. But rather than putting all your focus on what you cannot control, why not put it to better use? Where it can make an impact. You'll help your money more if you shift your attention to what you can do when it comes to your financial life, and this is where you can truly make a difference.

Staying focused on what you can control when it comes to your money builds confidence and a sense of empowerment. The same amazing confidence that I got to witness first-hand in Rachel's transformation. It helps you to create an action plan for your financial life. Because taking action is the only way to reach your financial goals. Rachel was able to incorporate actionable steps that were in her control in order to take charge of her financial life and you can too. Let's review areas of your financial life that you *do* have control over, and that deserve your valuable time and energy.

Creating and Building Your Empowerment Account

An "empowerment" account, or what is commonly referred to as an "emergency" account, covers expenses when unplanned events arise.

I choose to call it an empowerment account because I believe there's energy behind the words we use. And so I don't want the focus to be on a possible "emergency." Calling it an empowerment account feels much more positive. This way you can see it as extra money that gives you options. An empowerment account serves as safety net for you and your family. Life will always throw surprises your way, like when your cat thinks it's a good idea to swallow a sewing needle and needs emergency surgery to have it removed. And although you assumed cats were smarter than dogs when you opted for a family pet, what you can control is having additional money available at a moment's notice to cover the massive vet bill (and for all you cat lovers, I'm happy to report Katniss survived the surgery).

If you don't already have an empowerment account in place, no problem. But let's get you on track to setting one up now. It will ease your worries knowing you can support your family (and pets) through anything.

Here are a few key tips to building your surplus:

- Do what you can—anything is better than nothing when it comes to money. If you're looking to build your empowerment account but don't have much to spare, don't sweat it; do what's feasible for now. Even $25 a month or each paycheck will make a difference.
- Target at least three–six months' worth of expenses—if you're wondering how much surplus you should have, that depends. It's different for everyone, based on unique life circumstances. But aiming for three–six months' worth of your expenses is a good rule of thumb. If you have a dual income household, work in stable industries, and have no children, you might aim for the

lower end of the range. If you have children, are self-employed, are single, or work in a highly volatile industry, you might want to stick to the higher end of that range or even consider aiming for nine–twelve months' worth.

- Give it a special spot—your empowerment savings is meant to be easily accessible when you need it. But you also don't want it too accessible. You wouldn't want to unintentionally spend it or lose track of how much you've set aside by mingling it with your regular checking account. Ideally, you should set up a separate savings account. Bonus tip—also aim to earn some risk free return on the balance. Shop around at banks or investment companies to see who is offering the best interest on your cash.

- Get clear on the rules—this money will cover living costs or unplanned life expenses that come up. Don't get me wrong; a Peloton bike is a great personal investment—but you can save separately for fancy exercise equipment. Your empowerment account should be protected for true emergencies. So you can eliminate the stress of the unknown. If you have a partner, this is also a great opportunity to start a dialogue on what type of circumstances or expenses would qualify for tapping into this account to get on the same page.

Getting Invested and Staying Invested

You and I have no control over the performance of the stock markets. And what you hear from the financial professionals over and over again is the statement: "Time in the market is more important than *timing* the market." Although some still hold out hope that there might be some magic trick to transform their results. A common misconception about investing is that success lies in mastering the exact timing of when to invest. Finding and buying into investments at the absolute bottom, and selling when they hit their peak. Stock markets go up and they go down. Knowing this, you may deduce that if you invest right before they go up and exit before they go down, then this would be the best strategy to optimize your potential return. Unfortunately, this is oversimplifying the investment process and there's no crystal ball to tell you the exact opportune time to enter and to exit. Believe me, because if there was I'd be a billionaire, or out of a job.

Striving to produce this kind of result usually does more harm than good as you keep tinkering with your investments. The harsh reality is this: the markets are smarter than us and are usually many steps ahead of us. So if the plan is to pick your spot to buy or sell by keeping a close eye on things . . . at the point you see it happening, you've probably already missed the perfect moment.

If you're trying to buy at the bottom, you'll need to see the markets moving up before you can confirm that the bottom has indeed been reached, therefore missing the bottom.

If you're looking to sell at the top, you'll need to see the market move downward before you know what the ultimate top was.

Even by watching it like a hawk, you're still always coming from a place of reaction. This can result in buying into the markets once they have already moved up, and heading for the exits after they have already hit the bottom. And if that's the case, then you are essentially doing the exact opposite of the recommended—buy low, sell high.

I'm going to super-simplify the stock market here. If you zoom out and look at the long-term historical performance there are ups and downs, but the general direction is still an upward sloping line.

This is why we invest. Because despite the ups and downs of the stock markets, over the long term, markets have traditionally increased in value. The long-term upward progress has outpaced all dips and downward movements. The value of investing comes from being invested (to participate in the power of compounding, as discussed in Chapter 9). You cannot predict the peaks and valleys of the market with precision, so that's out of your control. But a better strategy, and one that you do have control over, is getting invested and staying invested.

This is especially important to remember when the markets are going down. There's a natural emotional response to do something when markets are heading in a negative direction. As you see the number decreasing in your investment accounts the urge to take control will be strongest at this point. But you cannot change the markets. And moments when you're feeling most out of control is the best time to shift your focus to what you can do, which in this case is often staying invested to take advantage of that long-term upward trajectory. You might even use the opportunity to add some more cash because who can resist a good sale?

Knowing you aren't expected to time the market should bring you a sense of relief. Making money your thing doesn't require becoming a stock picking guru that buys and sells stocks at the exact opportune moments. Ups and downs are going to happen, and guess what, they will probably surprise you each time. But you don't care because you know there's nothing you can do about that. What you can do is be invested and reap the rewards of compounding by giving your money lots of time to grow.

Living the Dream

You control the vision for your finances. Don't let your money boss you around. Playing defense and being at the mercy of your financial destiny may sound like:

- When can I afford to buy a home?
- Is it financially possible for me to take that dream trip?
- Are we (am I) in a secure enough financial position to support children?
- Will I ever be able to retire or will I have to work until I die?

Letting your money decide what's possible for you isn't the way to a fulfilling life. The best part about money is getting to envision what you're going to do with it. It's your money and you get to decide what's possible. This is where planning your financial future comes in. What are the things that you envision achieving, and getting to experience and to buy with your hard earned cash?

Get specific on your financial goals. Grab a pen and paper, or open up a Google doc and capture your goals in writing. If you're single, you're the boss. If you have a partner, make sure you each put down your own goals, as well as the ones you make as a team. As a minimum you'll want to answer the following questions for each goal:

1. What are you saving for?
2. How much will you need?
3. When will you need the money?

Get as detailed as possible with your vision. Write it all down, the more specific the better: where you are, what you're doing, the company you are with, what you're wearing, and is there ice cream? (Am I the only one that associates ice cream with financial freedom?)

There's no "one size fits all" approach to planning for your financial future, so dream big. You have control over planning for your goals and then seeing them through to execution making them a reality.

Keep in mind your goals today might change at different stages in your life and look different five, ten, twenty years from now. And that's completely okay. Nothing is set in stone when it comes to your financial future, so feel free to go back to review and update these anytime. But what doesn't change is that it's always up for to you to decide. Nobody gets to tell you what your financial future will be, only you control that, and the best way to see it through is to start with a goal.

Your Emotional Responses

The ebbs and flows of money can have you on edge of your seat. Especially when it comes all at once: you get the parking ticket, run out of gas, your dishwasher breaks down, and you need presents for five separate birthday parties your kid is invited to, all in one weekend! In these moments it's hard to feel in control of your money. Instead, you're convinced there's some sort of evil money force working against you.

Stay strong! There are still always things you can control in these moments. Look for them. Because forgetting that you're in control can lead to self-defeating behaviour such as emotionally driven spending splurges. Nothing good comes from accepting defeat, saying "screw it," and turning to your phone for an online shopping binge. Recognize that these are only moments or seasons, and they will pass.

There will be moments when it feels like you are taking five steps backward rather than making forward progress. But don't let them veer you off course completely. You still ultimately get to decide where your money goes. Thinking big picture might help smooth out some of these money blips. For instance, maybe you choose to scale back on some of the discretionary purchases when you know wedding season is coming up and you have loads of events to attend.

Celebrate Your Successes

Finding opportunities to celebrate is something you can control when it comes to your money. There should be no shortages of celebration throughout your journey. Money is a big part of life and a big responsibility; don't underestimate the hard work of adulting. The other day, when I woke up Ivy for school, very randomly the first words out of her mouth was the question "Do you have to pay bills *every* month, Mom, or just one time?" (Was she having money nightmares?)

My response, "Yes, *every* month, so enjoy being a kid while you can. You're lucky you get to spend your day at school with no expectations to bring in the big bucks."

Probably a bit more intense than I needed to be, but I've never claimed to be a morning person.

You pay your bills *every* month. You work your butt off clocking hours of overtime to get that promotion. You attempt to sell your bigger ticket items online to annoying strangers to try to recoup some costs. You walk past that new pair of Uggs because deep down you know yours are still in good shape. You search the freezer, with unwavering faith that there has to be something edible for dinner to keep that eating-out budget in line. Being a grown up in the money game isn't easy; you're amazing for all the work you do. Congratulations!

Don't let your hard work go unnoticed. Your efforts deserve to be celebrated. Balance out the work and sacrifices by rewarding yourself. But make sure you don't spend *any* money doing so . . . kidding, of course, you can spend money on celebrating your successes; I'm not that mean.

Giving yourself time to enjoy and have fun along the way is how you stay on course with your bigger money goals (like financial freedom) that might call for some major dedication. Say you've been on a roll with meals at home. Fabulous! Maybe a pizza takeout night for the family is in order. You've purged an abundance of junk and managed to make some money off it by having a garage sale. Awesome. Why not celebrate by pampering yourself a little with a new candle, book, or maybe a bottle of wine. You're ready to get serious about writing down your money goals? Now that's what I like to hear! Why not set yourself up for success by buying a fancy new luxurious money journal. And of course it can be larger rewards for bigger sacrifices as well. Maybe the whole family has been pitching in during those tough months of working toward a promotion and now its time to celebrate with a vacation.

If you don't make time to celebrate and enjoy the journey you are more likely to burn out or give up entirely. You cannot always control what life throws at you when it comes to finances, but being intentional about celebrating the hard work you do is something that is in your realm of control, and you deserve it.

Uncertainty is a key characteristic of money. Which I know sucks. *But* it's still possible to feel empowered and have unshakeable confidence about your money. Direct your efforts and energy to what you can control. Let go of the things you can't change and instead focus on what actions you *can* take for your money. Because taking action is confidence in motion and the first step toward your goals.

TAKING ACTION

Do one thing that's in your control toward a money goal you have:

Find out the price for that Hawaii vacation on your bucket list.
Open the account for your empowerment savings.
Make an extra payment on your credit card.
Put $50 into your retirement account.

CHAPTER 12

SPEND SOME TIME WITH YOUR MONEY AND GO ON A MONEY DATE

'VE SPENT A FAIR BIT of my adult life in the dating game looking for "the one." I was an early adopter of online dating, attended speed dating events, allowed myself to be set up on several blind dates, and took my trips to bars with friends extra-seriously by spending hours curling my hair. Unfortunately, nothing came from those efforts other than an array of comedic material about how bad a first date truly can be. I can look back now and laugh about those encounters, and share the age-appropriate stories with my daughter, her favorite being the greedy pizza guy that ate the entire pie to himself (didn't share a single piece with me). But I would be lying if I said these disastrous dates didn't leave me with an overall negative and hopeless view on dating. And it was likely that bias that led me to the period I stayed in for several years which I called—the *avoidance* phase.

At that time I had a lot on my plate anyway as a single parent and building my business, so saying I didn't have the time was an easy cover-up. During those years, I gave absolutely zero time and attention to finding a partner or being in a romantic relationship. And what did my nonexistent effort result in? You guessed it, being perpetually single. And I'm talking really, really single—not even one disastrous first date to speak of during those years.

I've done a lot of personal development work since then and I know now that if I truly want to find that special someone, I cannot avoid dating, relationships, and love. Finding a partner starts by being open, and giving that part of my life time and attention. It means seeing the possibilities, rather than burying myself under a pile of excuses.

And just like I hid from my love life, I see women take a similar approach when it comes to the relationship with their money. They enter their own period of avoidance, but in this case it's the money *avoidance* phase. They defend this choice with valid excuses, not unlike the ones I'd given when it came to dating.

Have you ever found yourself avoiding the topic of money? Maybe you've had good intentions to try but had some disappointing first experiences akin to my first dates. Perhaps you enrolled in a course or read a personal finance book but it didn't really resonate with you, searched for a financial professional to work with but couldn't find the right fit, attempted investing on your own but then gave up after seeing all the investment options, or opted to delete it from the to-do list when life got too busy. Avoidance is an easy solution to any tricky topic, especially money, which like finding love, can be uncomfortable, overwhelming, and stressful.

But if you have dreams for your future, ignoring your money will not get you any closer to achieving them. Neglecting your money will not progress you toward your end goals. In fact, it may actually take you further away from them as you money erodes away from inflation (talked about in Chapter 9).

Paying attention will help you achieve the unshakeable money confidence that is needed when money is your thing. It's about taking initiative, checking in on your cash, making adjustments where needed, and celebrating successes. Unfortunately the avoidance tactics play out all too often where people give very little or *no* time to their money. You exert so much of your precious energy into making money. Most of you probably spend upward of forty hours per week earning money, the majority of your waking hours. But do you spend any time working on your money?

With how much of yourself you give to earning it, doesn't that give your money the right to rank high on your list of priorities? Doesn't it deserve your time and attention?

Results happen when you can give your money the effort it deserves. This could look like:

- Reconstructing your beliefs around money with a more positive outlook, open to the possibilities
- Creating your wealth snapshot (outlined in Chapter 7)
- Understanding your spending habits
- Getting specific on exactly what you want to achieve with your money and writing it down
- Expanding your financial literacy
- Developing strong money communication with your partner
- Celebrating money milestones and successes

Doesn't this sound a bit more like what your money deserves?

For a reality check on how little time you may be giving your money, let's compare it to something fun and exciting that really gets your attention—like planning a vacation! How much time did you spend planning your last vacation? A day? A week? Now honest reflection moment: do you spend this much time planning as it relates to your money (which also happens to be the tool that makes your vacations possible)? I suspect it is the fun exciting stuff that gets a bit more of your time. And I get it; vacations are a blast. But there's a very real possibility you may be selling your money short.

Everyone could spare a little more time in their schedule for money matters. And there was a period when I too wasn't giving my money enough loving. Early on in my career I decided to enlist the support of a life coach—intuitively knowing my life was lacking balance. One of the initial exercises my coach had me complete was the wheel of life. The wheel was divided into slices like a pizza. Each slice being labeled with a category or area of one's life including family, relationships, money, business/career, health, personal growth, and social life/hobbies. The goal of the exercise is to gain insight from this visual tool of where you might be focusing the majority of your time and energy, and to identify the areas you may be neglecting. It aims to bring you back into balance. What I discovered after completing my own life wheel was that the vast majority of my focus was on my business/career and family (as a single momma) and very little was given to the money category. Seeing this was a big wake-up call for me. I was so passionate about helping other people in their financial lives but turns out I was not giving time and attention to my own. Discovering this early on was key because I developed an important relationship building strategy with my money. As a busy professional and parent the change for me came from being intentional about actually scheduling time to give to my own finances. And this was the start of my money dates!

"Money dates?" What the heck are those you may be wondering, envisioning a new dating app where you swipe for dollar bills. Sorry, no awkward first dates with a big pile of cash. My money dates were actually nonnegotiable and uninterrupted time that I devoted to my money. Just some special romantic quality time with my cash. For my money dates, I would block off a specific date and time in my calendar. The time was spent working on my own money. It started with one date, but my money and I hit it off so well that there were plenty more to follow. The focus of my first date was tracking expenses. As a new business owner there had been a lot of changes in spending, so doing this activity turned out to be very insightful. After tackling that first topic I was excited to take on the next which was setting up a plan for saving to fund my daughter's postsecondary education. After each date I felt a stronger connection with my money, and it felt *so* good to be taking actual action steps and getting things done. I was eager to plan and schedule the next date with my money; it was definitely love at first sight.

I've been successfully dating my money for several years now and it's something I highly recommend for all my clients to do too. And now I get to share this fabulous money habit with all you reading this as well! The biggest hurdle is scheduling in that first money date. You can come up with all sorts of excuses to put it off for another time and continue to avoid it. So I will try to make this easier for you, if you're new to money dates—my key dating tips are:

1. Actually book it in: Don't add it to a list of random tasks on a scrap of paper. Because then there's a better chance of you

organizing your sock drawer than setting your money date. Put it in your calendar as an event. Once it's in the calendar that's serious, you mean business, and you cannot stand up your money!

2. Create a recurring event: Ongoing maintenance is required. Don't be like twenty-year-old me who forgot about the importance of regular oil changes only to have the engine seize in my Dodge Colt. There are a lot of moving parts when it comes to your money, for best results it requires recurring check-ups or check-ins. This also removes any pressure because unlike a real first date you can guarantee there will be another one! So if you don't show up as your best, need a bit of a do over, or some more time, that's completely okay; you always have the next one. Choose a frequency that works for you—monthly tends to work best for me. But for you maybe it's a bit more often at the start if you have a lot of ground to cover, and then perhaps it decreases after that.

3. For singles—do it solo. For couples—do it together: What's great about a money date is that unlike a traditional date—it can be done solo! If you're single the money date will be some special time for you and your money. And if you're in a relationship a money date is most effective when done with your spouse or partner. This presents a fabulous opportunity to discuss money topics openly with each other. Financial topics are one of the leading causes of disagreements in relationships. A money date is a perfect opportunity for you to open the lines of communication and to get on the same page when it comes to your financial goals and dreams. You're both on the same team, and by working together you're setting yourselves up for success in reaching whatever goals you set out to achieve. If the relationship is new, a money date is a wonderful idea to incorporate when the time

is right. It's a less intimidating approach to discuss those money topics that may feel awkward or uncomfortable. Having it as a scheduled task sets the date and time where you both know that money will be the topic of conversation.

4. Make it fun: So you don't ghost your date; you want to make this time with your money something you look forward to. Do what you can to make it fun, because spending time with your money is awesome and it should feel good. Whether that's making your favorite tea, adding a sweet treat, playing a pump up playlist, or lighting incense to refresh your space. Whatever gets you amped up for the date and doesn't have you running for the exits is what matters (yes, I've resorted to fleeing the scene mid-date once or twice).

The above tips will help you set the date. But now what do you actually do on a money date, you may be wondering? It's not like you can take your bank account to dinner and a movie. Instead, I assign topics for my time with my money. Once you get into the habit and routine of paying attention to your money the topics of focus will likely start to flow to you as you get to know your money better. But of course, I want to set you up for success when it comes to spending time on your money.

Don't try to cram in too much on one date, take it slow, spending time with your money is something you are now striving to do on a regular basis, so there will always be another opportunity to pick up where you left off at your next date. Here are some money date ideas:

Getting to Know You Date

You'll want to set up your desk or kitchen table for this one. You can even light some candles, play some low music, and pour yourself a glass of wine if you like. Take an hour or two to go through the awareness tools you started in the Chapters 7 and 8. Really get to know your wealth snapshot to have a thorough understanding of where you stand. Share your dreams and desires for it (either with your partner, or you can write them down if you're doing this solo)—where would you like to see this wealth number next year and the year after.

Cheap Date

Think of going Dutch, getting creative with a low cost or no cost activity, or taking your date to McDonald's (oh, I wouldn't mind that one bit). Now look at your expenses with this lens. Are there ways you can cut costs? What could you do without?

It's become very easy to spend money. Online shopping allows you to make purchases right from the comfort of your home with the click of a button. Targeted marketing literally reads your mind and knows exactly what ads to serve you. Social media puts on display fabulous lifestyles that leave you envying what others have. And to make matters worse you don't even need any money to get everything your heart desires thanks to the accessibility of debt. With all these forces at work it's far easier to spend than to save. Having a cheap date is an opportune time to create a spending plan for your ideal money scenario. The easiest side to tackle on the income and expenses equation is usually the expenses as you can implement changes immediately. Use this date to brainstorm ideas to spend less.

Get resourceful and do what is realistic for you when it comes to cutting costs. Here are a few ideas to get those creative juices flowing on where to save some cash:

- Skip a few: Let those roots get a tad more length by getting your hair done four times per year versus six, for instance.
- Take out the trash: Get rid of anything that can be easily eliminated right now, like subscriptions to streaming services or apps you aren't using.
- Be a little less classy: Instead of buying your fancy lattes daily, can you limit it to a few days per week, and attempt to be your own Barista the other days?
- Follow the money: Try recording every single purchase you make for one full week to get very clear on your spending habits.
- Dolla bills: When is the last time you used *real* money? Give yourself a certain cash budget for the week or month, when the money runs out, no more spending (yes, I am talking about real paper money here).
- Lay down the law: Try setting money rules or boundaries for yourself. For instance any purchase over $150 you wait on and think about for 48 hours.

During this money date, pick one to two of these strategies (or come up with some of your own), and plan how you'll incorporate them over the coming weeks or months.

Wealthy Woman Date

Do you ever feel guilty that you don't save enough money? If so, devoting time and attention to developing a savings strategy on your money date is time well invested. Even if you're already saving, there's no harm in saving more; it just means more money for you! A higher savings rate can lead to achieving your financial freedom goals sooner, creating a nice cash safety net, or even building a wonderful travel account for a dream adventure. Adding a portion of your income to savings each month is how you become a super saver. But as for "how much?" that will depend on your unique circumstances and goals. Most importantly, do what works for you. Setting attainable savings targets will ensure you don't set yourself up for failure. A commonly cited rate for your long-term financial freedom goal is to save 10–15% of your gross income. This number will depend on a variety of factors such as your age and desired lifestyle in retirement. So when it comes to saving there's no "one size fits all" solution. But the more you save the quicker you build wealth. If you're looking for some inspiration to up your savings rate, below are a few ideas:

- *Anything* is better than nothing. Do what you can even if it doesn't feel like much.
- Implement cost cutting (what you found on your cheap date).
- Make it easy; don't give yourself an extra task; set it to automatically add to your savings when you get paid. Pay yourself first!
- Increase your savings when you get a pay raise or bonus.
- Maximize any employer plans and matching programs available to you.

- Set targets and make them specific. It's much more motivating to work toward a goal, such as "I currently save 5% of my income but I will increase that to 7% by the end of this year."

Study Buddies Date

When it comes to making money your thing, learning is part of the journey. But learning can be fun too. Having study buddies made cramming for an exam much more fun during my business school days. So invite your partner, spouse, or a friend or family member along as this money date is an opportunity to teach and learn together. First step is for you and your study buddy to choose a money or finance topic that you want to learn more about (focus on the same topic or each choose a different one). For instance let's say you choose inflation. Leading up to this date, each spend time researching and learning about inflation. When you come together for the big date you get to take turns teaching each other about inflation. Learning through reading or listening is great. But if you can then take those lessons and teach it to someone else it builds a deeper knowledge and understanding of the concept. This date is a fabulous long-term investment in yourself, and you both walk away learning something new so it's a win-win!

Blind date

I'm sure you would all rather have a fun date than a serious one. But dealing with the tough stuff is important in relationships, and it's important for your money as well. When it comes to your money you might have the best laid plans, but even the most air tight strategy can go astray. This date is all about planning for the unknown, so when stuff comes up you are ready to take it on. Because you're dealing with the unknown and worst case scenarios this money date topic might feel uncomfortable and awkward at first, but it's still important to have. Whether single or in a relationship, this is about asking the hard questions. Like, what if:

- You were seriously injured?
- You were diagnosed with an illness?
- You developed a disability that impacted your ability to work?
- You or your partner were to pass away unexpectedly?
- You divorced/separated?

This is a chance to ensure the proper supports are in place to protect yourself and your family from the unexpected. Important items include reviewing insurance policies, having a will done or updating your will if it's not current, having a plan in place if you have minor children, updating beneficiary designations, and having or building an empowerment account. It might feel difficult to approach these topics at first. But once you've done the work to protect yourself from the unknown it feels like a weight has been lifted. And I don't at all want to downplay the heaviness of this topic so do make sure you reward yourself for taking on the awkward blind date. A reward could be binge watching your favorite show, ordering in from your favorite sushi spot, or a bubble bath—whatever it takes to give yourself the congrats you deserve.

These are a few topics to get you started with money dates, but the possibilities are endless. What matters most is that you're spending quality time with your money giving it the attention and care it deserves. This is nothing like going on the date with some guy you swiped right to. A money date is akin to spending time with your soulmate. And if you play your cards right on your money date you'll be guaranteed a lifelong partner that makes your dreams a reality.

TAKING ACTION

Open your schedule and book a money date right now! Or even better, drop everything and have one! Pick from the date suggestions in the chapter or design one of your own.

CHAPTER 13

OUT WITH THE OLD, MAKE WAY FOR THE NEW MONEY BOSSES

HAVE YOU EVER HAD a conversation that you can recall so vividly because of how impactful it may have been in your life? There's one that happened early on in my career in the finance industry. It's been burned in my brain. Stored in my memory as one of the stupidest things a male colleague has ever said to me.

It started like this: In my early days in the business prior to my start as an advisor, I had been working as an associate to a financial advisor. But I was reassigned (demoted) to a floater at the firm because the advisor I was working with decided he no longer had use for me on his team (aka he felt threatened that the clients had taken a strong liking to me). My first task was to assist Tom, another advisor who had been left to fend for himself when his associate Charlotte found a welcoming and supportive team to join at a competing firm.

My joy for her escape was short lived when I realized I would be her temporary replacement.

As soon as I sat down at the desk that still housed some snack remnants left behind from her quick exit, I knew I was in for a treat. Tom was one of the old timers in the industry, who started his business in the early days when advisors would "dial for dollars" using a phone book to find new clients.

As I lowered Charlotte's chair so my feet could touch the floor, which is a typical problem when you're five-foot-two, I noticed the massive stack of papers in front of me. Through the glass walls of his office, Tom appeared to be unoccupied, so I grabbed a notebook and pen in hopes to get some guidance because despite his assumption I was not a mind reader.

After knocking lightly, he waved me in. I stood before him at his massive desk as there were no chairs for guests. Then he gestured behind me. I turned to see a large brown couch that in no way could be classified as office furniture. It looked like it had spent years in a house of roommates and then should have been let go with a *free* sign on it. I'm no couch snob by any means but that couch had no place in an office. It didn't even seem hygienic to sit down on. So I perched on the edge and missed the entire beginning of what Tom was saying because all that I was thinking about was how in the world this rugged, out-of-place couch was even allowed on the 41st floor of this swanky office tower.

The important part of this conversation came when Tom asked my career plans, and how long I would be working with him. It might have been the feeling of being taken back in time and among old friends sitting on that dumpy couch that took over but I felt comfortable and compelled to tell him the truth. I shared that in all honesty, I was actively searching for other employment. I confessed my dream of becoming a financial advisor to this complete stranger, and shared that the recent demotion at the office and arrival of my daughter were the catalysts that inspired me to start making my dream a reality. At that point I was hoping he would congratulate me or perhaps offer some words of encouragement and advice being that once upon a time he too built his business from scratch.

But instead Tom responded, "A woman cannot succeed as a financial advisor in Calgary. The majority of the wealth in this city is held by oil and gas executives who are men, and they wouldn't invest their money with a woman."

I sat on Tom's terrible couch eyes wide in shock. His statement was beyond inappropriate and insensitive. And shone a spotlight on the painfully outdated views that clearly still exist when it comes to money and investing.

That moment was one of the most impactful in my career because it was when I knew it was time for me to prove the Toms of the world wrong. The archaic view that wealth is only concentrated with men as the breadwinners and top executives is completely false. And his doubt in the capabilities of women to manage money was also ridiculous.

The next day I selected the thirty-minute option on the parking meter knowing I would be brief. I marched into the branch manager's office and informed him that I *quit*. It was never clearer to me that my plan to support women investors needed to begin right away. I immediately started reaching out to all the investment firms to pitch my plan.

As I can personally attest to, these ideas around wealth don't make it any easier for women to make money their thing. The male-centric view of wealth is based on the patriarchal past of men going to work while women stayed at home tending to the household duties and children. Anyone can easily see this is no longer the case. And has not been for some time now. But views around money and building wealth have not caught up with the times—and Tom was the proof of this.

I had a review meeting with a lawyer client recently and her biggest concern was that she made more money than her fiancé, and she was perplexed about what to do about that. I told her that she should be very proud of achieving this success in her career and she deserved to be well compensated for it.

And that was it. There was no problem to be solved. There was nothing she needed to "do" about it—it was just the way it was, and that was awesome. The reality is that more women each year are becoming the primary breadwinner in their family. Times have changed and how the world views the wealth of women must change as well to keep up.

I have the opportunity to work with women that have some very impressive salaries. I get to see firsthand examples of women making *big* money on a regular basis, and I'm blessed for that because it's helped me stretch my own goals of what is possible.

I spoke to a client a few weeks ago that let me know her revenue for her small business was on track to hit one million this year. And I know that she will indeed hit her goal because her whole being exuded so much confidence and assurance when she shared these details in our financial strategy session.

Guess what that means, Tom? Women *do* have money!

A woman may earn more than her spouse/partner, she may earn the same, or she may earn less. And she could also be the sole financial provider in a partnership or independently. Many scenarios exist. And whatever that looks like for you, embrace it. The important point is for you to own your role as a serious earner. You cannot undermine your contribution, no matter what amount.

Make way for powerful change when women stop devaluing themselves and their financial contributions. Change in the distribution of household duties, in who leaves work to pick up a sick kiddo from school, and in financial decision making for the family.

Major benefits to women embracing their roles as serious financial contributors that stand out in my mind are expediting equal pay, and more women embracing financial independence.

Women Getting PAID

If you want more money, it's up to you to ask for it. As much as you hope your boss would walk up to you with a pile of cash for all your extra hard work that usually isn't how it plays out. Pay negotiations generally start by the employee taking the initiative to have the uncomfortable conversation. A conversation that women tend to view as more painful than a bikini wax. And just like it might be easier to weigh other options for hair removal (like buying the swimsuit cover up), you may lean toward the pain-free scenarios to your salary woes. Like avoiding the conversation altogether. If women simply accept where things stand and don't ask for more, then guess what—they don't get more. Women still on average earn less than men, so we need to take action if we want to see this change. When women see their contributions as having an impact on the family finances they may be more inclined to rip off that strip and initiate the salary conversations.

Women Embracing Independence

The typical stereotype of men being the breadwinners can leave women feeling vulnerable and at the mercy of someone else to make their financial goals possible. How many women still believe that they have to marry an old rich guy if they are going to have a lot of money? If there's even one, that's too many. Because the answer should be none. No woman should think that she needs to choose a wealthy partner or a man with good earnings potential in order for her to have money.

I never want my Ivy, my daughter, to grow up thinking that achieving her goals depends on having the financial support of a man. I want Ivy to know it's possible for her to achieve any financial dream she sets out achieve, that she has the power to make it happen. Even if she has mentioned she wants to be an artist, she will be a darn prosperous one!

Holding on to the old ideals that were prevalent when women didn't go into the workforce and weren't in charge of finances will only hold us back. There's power to throwing out these dated stereotypes. It can expedite equal pay. And it can affect positive and healthy conversations about finances in relationships based in equality. Women need to be comfortable and proud about being serious earners, and embrace the decision making power this brings. Women can and should take on a leadership role with their finances.

I'm giving all women reading this book a promotion right now, and it's a big one.

From this point forward you are the chief executive officer (CEO) of your money—aka you are the *Money Boss*.

Does the boss position sound overwhelming/intimidating? If so, no problem. I've got you. I want to set you up for success by sharing some tips on being the best money boss you can be. I know you're capable of excelling in the role; you are reading this book after all. You already have the makings of a money boss. So here are my top tips for being the best darn boss you can be:

- Practice patience—Maybe you're feeling amped and ready to suit up in this new, but I want to remind you this is a long-term position. A lifelong one in fact. Money is an everyday part of grown up life. You want to make sure you go easy with this new boss role and set realistic expectations of yourself so you don't burn out. Be kind to yourself. Ease yourself into the position. Maybe your first order of business is to finish reading this book. Great leaders take a long-term approach because empires are built over time and overnight success stories aren't the norm. When it comes to money, patience is vital because although compounding is pretty magical, watching it do its thing on a daily basis is about as exciting as watching paint dry. Patience is essential for persisting through the ups and downs that come with being a money boss, and for seeing positive results toward your biggest goals.

- Conquer the fear—Easier said than done, I know. But one of the biggest factors I see holding women back when it comes to making money—and I can't stress this enough—their thing is *fear*. Fear is normal, especially when it comes to things that are new, different, and uncomfortable. And money can encompass all those. Conquering your fear is so *rewarding*. Money confidence and empowerment live on the other side of fear. You so deserve that, and I want it for you more than anything. I get to see firsthand the payoff for brave women who've embraced being a money boss. These women are setting big money goals for themselves—hitting seven figure revenues in their business, building million-dollar dream homes, travelling the world and staying in fabulous accommodations, and getting to quit their jobs to enjoy an early retirement. These are all real examples from the clients I work with. They took their financial dreams to reality and you can do that too. But I can tell you one thing these women had in common; they didn't let fear hold them back when it came to building wealth and going after what they wanted. And this doesn't mean that fear didn't come up for them; these women weren't simply born money masters. They encountered unknowns along the way but didn't let the fear take over. One had to navigate an uncomfortable conversation about setting up a cohabitation agreement with her partner as she knew the value of protecting her assets after her first marriage ended in divorce. But it turned out to be the best thing she could've ever done when it saved her from losing half of her assets which she has continued to build into multimillions. Another quit her stable employment position to take a leap of faith and start a business based on an innovative technology. Which she has now built into a multimillion dollar internationally recognized company. Fear will come up. But if you face it head on and work through it rather than let is scare you away, then you get to build the money confidence required of a money boss.

- Get curious—There's no such thing as dumb questions as it relates to your wealth. I stress this in my business at any opportunity I get, when meeting with new clients, teaching courses, or presenting at seminars. I truly urge you to ask anything when it comes to money. Don't. Hold. Back. As much as I try to be super aware of how I explain money and investing topics, like most financial professionals I too, I am guilty of using financial jargon. So don't hold back; never feel intimidated to ask. And chances are if you don't know the answer you aren't the only one. By getting curious and asking questions you're benefiting the collective by building knowledge that you can then share with others.

- *What's the difference between a stock and a bond?*
- *How can I tell what I'm paying for my investments?*
- *What happens if I don't pay off my credit card each month?*
- *Why do they call it a bull or bear market?*
- *How is interest earned on my money?*
- *What's diversification?*
- *What is the stock market?*
- *What's the difference between the types of investment accounts? And which should I have?*

Whatever questions, don't hold back; ask away. Get curious. Take it all in and then share with others in your social circle. The best bosses are great mentors that strive to better everyone around them.

- Ditch the perfectionist—You'll never be perfect in the money game, so don't waste your energy trying to be. Even the greatest investors of all time had plenty of learning moments (screw ups) to share about their journeys. And I mean even the Warren Buffett's of the world don't claim to always be right. Guess what that means—you're among good company and you too are going to screw up! Mistakes will be made and your financial life might feel messy at times. The more you're able to accept this fact the more equipped you'll be to fail fast and get right back to it.

Successful investors don't let the failures take them out. They learn, and move on. Good bosses know that perfection is unrealistic; instead they are experts at being unshakable and know how to persevere and move forward in the face of adversity.

- Be open to learning—(remember Chapter 6) Successful leaders spend time investing in themselves through personal development. The same is true for you as a money boss; to be your best you'll have to be open to learning. Learning something new takes time, but the return on your investment is something that you can keep forever. The greatest leaders have an awareness of their strengths and their weaknesses. They can accept that they don't know it all, and can't be an expert at everything, but still they are open and willing to challenge themselves to learn something new.

- Don't play small—Set *big* goals for yourself. Playing small is boring. Money can and should be exciting! I know you have a big vision for yourself and your financial future. It might be the dreams you don't tell a soul about because they sound unrealistic and you're scared to be judged by others. So what it is? Maybe it's an oceanfront house in Malibu, or to be financially independent and able to retire at a ridiculously early age, or maybe like my daughter you want to own every single American Girl doll that exists (although I hope she grows out of that goal). Whatever it is, don't downplay it or trade it in for something smaller. You're the boss now, you get to decide what you're going for, and nobody gets to crush your dreams. Embrace the biggest money goals and let those be your inspiration for making money your thing!

To be unshakeable on this journey to building confidence I urge you to step into the role of CEO of your money. There's no reason why all women shouldn't be in a leadership position of their money. Let's celebrate women earning lots of money, women are breadwinners too, and it's important for them to have the CEO skills to look after their wealth.

Embrace your right to feel financially empowered. And hopefully these tips have made the whole "boss" title less intimidating or overwhelming. I'm so passionate about you feeling confident when it comes to your financial life.

You certainly are a Money Boss!

TAKING ACTION

Let's prove how competent and capable you are of being the CEO of your money. Identify your leadership strengths and write down instances of when you demonstrated those in your life:

Examples:

I have a positive attitude—when Ivy refuses to go to school I'm quick to point out how soon until the weekend! Even when it is just Monday!

I'm determined—when I was told by terrible Tom I couldn't succeed as an advisor; well, that added fuel to my fire and I kept going and going, and I did it!

I have the ability to inspire—when I do my workout in the evening right in front of the television Ivy gives up trying to catch a glimpse of her show through my shoulder presses and joins me!

Now that you remember how much of a boss you are, make one executive money decision.

Example:

Make a decision about monthly bills? Cancel a subscription or schedule an automatic retirement savings deposit!

PART 4

EMPOWERED YOU:
MONEY *IS* YOUR THING

CHAPTER 14

IT'S OKAY TO LIKE MONEY; YOU MAY EVEN GROW TO LOVE IT

YOU'VE COMMITTED TO making money your thing, but I must ask: Does the title of this chapter make you squirm a little inside?

What would your reaction be if someone announced: "I love money!"

How about if you said "I love money" out loud right now? How does that make you feel?

Is it awkward or uncomfortable to confess a love for your money? Or perhaps you're worried it sounds greedy or materialistic.

Nobody wants to be labeled as having either of those qualities. Greed and materialism are not exactly desirable traits. Society pressures women to be selfless and giving, which is much more "ladylike." The phrase "I love money" doesn't exactly exude altruism.

And so you're left in a tough spot. Yearning for an abundant life, all geared up to make money your thing. But unable to reconcile how to love your money without being judged.

It's a crappy and confusing place to be.

And I don't want you to spend another minute in that dilemma. It's time for a change. It's time for you to give yourself permission to *like* money. And from there, you may even grow to love it!

Part of making money your thing involves a healthy relationship with it, and love is the key ingredient to any strong and lasting connection.

My goal is for you to fully and unapologetically embrace *money love* by the end of this chapter. And to do that I think the best place to start is with my own confession, which is this!

I LOVE Money!

And I've loved it for a very, *very* long time. My mom asked me at the age of four what I wanted to do when I grew up. "I want to collect money," I said. She laughed at my goal and told little four-year-old me that I was describing a bank.

Although she didn't take my money career path seriously at that time, it didn't stop the passion I had for money. A few years later, I went on to become the designated coin roller in my family. This started when my piggy bank was getting full, and my mom pointed out that paying for things with a pile of change was time consuming and rather annoying to cashiers. She suggested I count my coins, put the correct number in the coin wrappers, and exchange them at the bank for bills. She kindly went to the bank to get me some paper rolls for each coin denomination.

She showed me how to stack the coins and roll them in paper, just like I was wrapping a present.

A money present! Those light brown wrappers were a game changer.

I loved rolling money.

I would sort, count, and stack the coins in smaller piles before combining enough of the small stacks into a larger tower that would be enough to fill the roll. When I didn't have enough of a particular coin, I kept an ongoing tally of how many I still needed to completely fill the roll. The minute I hit the target, I would get to rolling.

I was living my four-year-old dream, becoming the bank my mom had once told me I was describing.

Around the age of seven, on a weekend visit to my aunt Judy's home, I noticed a massive bucket full of change on the dresser in her bedroom. My eyes lit up. Christmas had come early. She had more coins than I had ever seen in my entire life. I *had* to roll those coins! I needed to be the first to know how much her treasure amounted to.

I did my best to hold in my bursting excitement when I politely asked Aunt Judy, "Can I pleeeeeeease roll your change?"

"Sure," she responded, much more easily than I expected.

And not only did she say yes *but* she also said she would *pay* me for offering to take on this big task. I'd hit the jackpot. I was going to get my hands on all that change, and she was going to pay me for doing what I loved.

Dreams do come true.

It took what felt like an entire day to roll all those coins. My fingers were sore and covered in a dusty film that gave them a sour iron-like smell. But that didn't matter; it was a small sacrifice for doing the most important job in the world. And I was rewarded at the end of my hard day's work with a $20 bill.

Coin rolling was only the beginning of my passion for money. I also fell in love with the game Monopoly after my cousin Michael introduced me to it around that same time. At family gatherings, he and I always found a suitable quiet spot to set up our game, which would go on for hours. And you'd better believe I was always the banker.

And then of course there were the small businesses I started early on, when I was still too young to be legally employed. One such venture involved capitalizing on a snow day when school was canceled. As soon as I found out the news, I seized the opportunity to shovel sidewalks for money. My friend Catherine joined as my business partner.

To put that snow dump into context, I'm talking well over 4 feet of snow (almost my height at the time). We were paid big bucks for clearing those sidewalks because it took well over an hour per house.

The love I had for money started early. And naturally, I assumed all people felt the same way about it. Imagine my surprise many years later as a financial advisor, when I started meeting with women to talk about their money, and they didn't share my enthusiasm.

I was intrigued by how they talked about their money. Or should I say, the way they *didn't* talk about money. Sitting across the table from these women to discuss their finances, what I witnessed time and again was their hesitation to *really* talk about their money.

They spoke about it in a strange sort of code, as if they'd been tasked with the challenge to refrain from saying the words—*money, wealthy, rich,* or *millionaire.*

It especially made for a challenging communication dynamic when I was meeting with a potential client for the first time. At this initial sit-down the objective is to learn more about their personal money goals. But that level of discovery is nearly impossible to do when the topic of their money is under lock and key.

At one particular meeting with a young female lawyer named Julie, her level of secrecy was so intense that I found myself feeling like I'd been transported into a spy movie. As our conversation progressed, she leaned in further and further while her voice got quieter until it became almost a whisper.

I was sure she had been tipped off that someone might be listening through the walls of the conference room, spying on this top-secret meeting.

But if someone was actually eavesdropping on that conversation, they wouldn't have a clue what we were talking about because she was doing such a good job of skating around the topic of money. As if it were a swear word.

When I created the business plan for my female-focused advisory practice, I'd envisioned myself having long conversations about money with other women. I imagined exploring a shared enthusiasm over money. Talking about big goals to building wealth and achieving major money milestones.

But after starting my business and meeting with all these women, what I actually found was that the vast majority of them didn't ever express outwardly wanting to "be rich" or "become a millionaire." In fact, out of the hundreds of women I met with early in my career there was only one that explicitly stated—"I want to be a millionaire by the time I turn 40." And that woman was Grace.

At first, Grace's statement caught me off guard, since I'd grown accustomed to using the secret language of money with women up until that point. I was still a new advisor at the time so I was inclined to concede and follow their lead. I had pushed aside the dreams I had for the *fun money chats,* and instead decided keep my money love hidden so I wouldn't scare them away.

But when Grace said those words about wanting to be a millionaire, I quickly perked up. My first reaction was to jump from my seat and start cheering, but I held it together and let my enthusiasm radiate through a big smile instead. I was so proud that she knew exactly what she wanted. She was sure of herself, and her goals. And completely unapologetic.

Grace loved money, exactly like me.

Meeting Grace reignited the spark I'd had when I started my businesses. I'd almost lost faith, and fell for the myth that women didn't care about money.

Her very specific big goal of becoming a millionaire by forty had me motivated to get to planning on how to get her there. We started by taking an inventory of where she stood with her finances (her wealth snapshot). She was in her early thirties, so she had less than ten years to get there, which wasn't a huge amount of time. But she had a good base of savings as her starting point, she was willing to get invested, she was in a career that offered yearly salary increases, and she was ready to up her savings game to make this happen.

I pulled out my favorite tool—the trusty financial calculator—and projected what she would need to put away each month to get to her goal. I created a plan designed around her target, including the investment strategy for the compounding growth rate that would help get her there. Next I set up the monthly savings to be pulled from her bank account, which would increase coinciding with her annual pay raises.

And like that, Grace was off to the races. Her million-dollar goal was in motion by her taking action and executing on the plan. It starts by allowing yourself to speak up about your money dreams with conviction like Grace did, only then can you take the steps to make them a reality. Nothing good comes from holding back and keeping those inner money dreams a secret.

In my love for talking all things money, I also created a podcast, *The Wealth and Wellness Podcast with Kalee Boisvert*, to encourage healthy conversations around wealth and promote positive relationships for women with their money. A recent guest shared that she'd also uncovered this phenomenon of women being afraid to love money (or maybe just afraid to say it out loud). In the episode, my guest Tammy shared that in her presentations geared toward empowering women, she gets the women in the audience to yell, "I love money."

She says the first time she asks them to do this she can sense the hesitation in the room. But by the end of her session, after she has shared the importance of women embracing their right to a wealthy life, she calls on the audience to yell it once more.

The second time she asks, the neighboring buildings can hear it.

If you're holding on to the belief that loving money is an undesirable trait, it's time to ditch that limiting thought like you did with the rest of them in Chapter 1. *Money* isn't a dirty word. Embrace it, talk about it, and say you *love it*.

Now, for Tammy, I want you to yell out loud, right now, "I love money."

This might feel awkward at first, and that's okay. But try it on; try to say it with more frequency until it starts to feel comfortable.

Affirming this statement out loud is a fabulous start to loving your money. But saying the words can only get you so far. You must also live and embody this relationship with your money to give true meaning to the words.

True love of your money will align your actions with these words. I'm eager to share some ideas that will move you into taking loving action for your money. But first, let's examine some of the common counterproductive behaviors that could be standing in the way of showing your money some love:

- Ignoring it: Taking a head in the sand approach, or simply doing nothing with your money is no way to show love. Loving relationships are based on getting to know and understand the other party.

- Burning through your cash: Making impulse purchases on meaningless items shows a disregard for your money. When you love something, you don't throw it away.

- Dodging debt: Continuing to build up credit card debt and hold balances on your card(s) with no plan to pay them down is not a loving strategy. The banks and other interest collectors get all the love from your money in these instances, and you're left paying the bill.

- Forgetting to save: Skipping savings sends the message that you don't want your money to accumulate into more, to continue to grow. And more money means even more to love.

- Mean girl self-talk: Getting caught up in guilt, shame, blame, or embarrassment can cast an overall negative energy for your money. Positivity breeds a loving money vibe.

Above are some of the most common unloving ways I see people engaging in with their money.

Now it's time to talk about how you can give your money some loving.

One of the most important ways you can embody love for your money is to not give it all away. When you love something, you keep it close. Holding it near and dear to your heart. The same is true with money. You cannot say you love money in one breath and then give it all away in the next. Life is expensive I know, and with an endless list of purchases, it can be easy to succumb to this distribution of your money to everyone else but yourself.

To show your money you love it, you must find ways to keep as much of it as you can. This concept of holding back some of your money for you also embodies the common personal finance tip: pay yourself first. If each month or each pay period you can designate a portion of your earnings to *you* first, then you are the true recipient of your hard-earned cash. Keeping a portion of what you earn is vital; it's the only way to build wealth.

If what you earn is entirely distributed to paying others with only enough to spare to have a few lattes and splurge a little on that Botox touch-up, this creates a powerful message about your money. The message: your money doesn't belong to you, and you must give it all away.

If you keep some of your own money at each pay period you have the power to change that message. By keeping a portion of what you earn, the action becomes a loving one—exemplifying how much you cherish it and want it to stick around.

The math is simple. If all your money (or more—which puts you into debt) goes out the door each month, you can't grow your fortune because there's simply nothing left. But if you direct a portion of what you earn to any type of savings (vacation fund, empowerment surplus, investment account, registered savings plan, tax-free savings account, etc.), you'll get closer to your wealth goals and show love and appreciation for your money.

If you're earning money, there's a disciplined savings strategy that's realistic for you. Whether it's once per month or every two weeks, keep it simple and set aside a portion of what you earn to pay yourself first. If you're new to saving, it might feel like a slow start, but you'll be surprised at how fast it adds up. No amount is too small because every bit adds to your money love bank. Watching your savings grow from this disciplined, consistent behavior is motivating and will hopefully inspire you to continue to add more.

Now that you're accumulating the savings, you might be wondering, what's next?

If you let your money pile up and do nothing, you could be missing out on fabulous opportunities. And you should always want what's best for the things you love. For it to excel you must give your money a purpose and a destination.

A great example of this was when my client, Laura, shared the breakdown of all her separate accounts for her money. What really stood out was how she took the extra step to be very intentional by giving each bucket of savings a name. Her accounts were broken down as follows (side note she wasn't being charged separate fees for each account, so that's one caveat to making various accounts— ensure your bank doesn't charge for each one):

- Checking account
- Milo account (she was a proud doggy momma)
- New car account
- Fun money
- Financial freedom

I loved how specific she was about directing her money to its proper location. There wasn't just a pile of surplus savings. Her money had a purpose and she made it easy to tell exactly what that was. Now that's money love.

Beyond giving your money direction, you must also put it to work. If you let it sit idle, it will never grow to its full potential. And love is not about keeping something small and holding it back. Your money deserves to grow and flourish, and you can achieve this by putting it to work. One of the best ways to do this is to invest it (as discussed in Chapter 9). When you invest your money, you give it the greatest opportunity to grow and compound. And I don't know about you, but multiplying money sounds like *lots* of love to me!

I'm optimistic you're now a believer in the power of loving your money. And how you can go about showing it that much-needed love with the actions to match.

Time for the best part. Let's talk about the magic of what happens when you start to love your money:

- You welcome in more of it: When you get to a place of truly accepting that you're allowed to love money, you open the doors to attracting more. Letting yourself love money means you also feel worthy and deserving of it. This sense of worthiness can be your biggest ally when you negotiate that well deserved raise, land a new client, or score a major bonus at work. When you exude a loving energy for your money, there's no stopping the flow. Sit back and watch how it keeps on finding its way to you. How could it not? You are a money magnet now!

- You stop second-guessing: When you allow yourself to fall in love you're trusting money, what it can do for you, and how it can work in your life. Knowing your money is there for you provides the reassurance to go after what truly feels right. You release yourself from criticism and self-sabotaging thoughts, instead trusting in all the good that's possible.

- You embrace independence: Money love is empowering. When you make sure you keep some by paying yourself first, you build wealth. This creates independence and financial freedom. You don't need to depend on someone else to make your financial goals a reality because you've collected your own pile of money. So now the only question is, what will you do with it?

- You've got more to give: Let's face it; giving feels good. And if this chapter has made you concerned that loving money means no more giving, well, don't you worry because that's not the case. But it's important to recognize that you cannot give if you're depleted. Keeping more and being diligent with building your wealth means you'll have more to give now that it's coming from a full tank.

- You build self-love: Choosing to love your money is a form of self-love that trickles into other aspects of your life too. Money love is about putting yourself first and prioritizing your needs. It's easy to get caught up looking at what others have and thinking you need the same to achieve happiness. Having your own personal loving relationship with money calls you to go within and focus on your own financial dreams. Self-love is the foundation of who you are, so honor it by letting your relationship with money support it.

And now that I've shared some of the many benefits that come with loving your money, I hope you too are feeling those loving vibes. And remember, it's *not* greedy or selfish to love it. Loving your money is empowering.

TAKING ACTION

Write Your Money Love Story

Spend time visualizing or writing down your thoughts or specifics about why you love money and what you are most grateful for.

A few examples:

I love money because it funded my beautiful wedding to my soulmate. It created the most magical day that we were able to enjoy with our friends and family on the beach in Hawaii and I am so grateful for this experience that I will never forget.

Or maybe,

I love my money because it supports my independent lifestyle. I know that I earn enough to be able to completely support myself and I don't have to rely on someone else to make my financial dreams a reality. I desire to find a partner in life and I am happy to bring positive money vibes and a positive money mindset to the relationship (no money baggage here!).

CHAPTER 15

IT'S MORE THAN JUST MONEY

Y OU'RE READING AN ENTIRE book about money and you've committed to making money your thing, and now I want to share something that may throw you for a loop.

Money is *nothing* in and of itself.

What if I told you I would give you $1 million dollars today, right now, transferred to your bank account, free and clear? You're an instant millionaire!

Now, how are you feeling about this windfall of cash with no strings attached? Are you excited? Relieved? Anxious? *Blissful!*

Before you get too carried away with your plans to be sipping margaritas on the beach or cruising your swanky Mercedes down Rodeo Drive, I forgot to mention there's a catch—you can't spend it. Not one cent of it. Your million-dollar gift must remain in your account untouched, forever.

Whaaaaaaaaat?!

You may be thinking; well, then take your million dollars back because it's useless to me. And you're correct to feel betrayed because what good would money be under that restriction? Your reaction proves that money itself isn't worth anything. Money only really matters when it has value, when you can use it. And if that's the case, then it's not money that will have an impact on your life; it's what you can do with your money that matters.

When you see money in this new light, you can dig deeper on this journey into what you truly desire. You can replace the word *money* with the values that you hold dear. And then money is no longer the motivating force, but achieving the life of your dreams is the key driver. Achieving more of what you want (freedom, travel, fancy dinners out), and less of what you don't want (stress, debt, having ramen noodles for dinner every night).

You don't long to curl up in pile of newly minted dollar bills, unless you're Scrooge McDuck that is. And making it rain with a stack of cash can only entertain you for so long. A more important question to ask yourself is this: What is it that you want from money?

- To travel the world?
- To build a comfortable home with plenty of space for your family?
- An early retirement?
- A quick exit from your job to pursue your life passion?
- Unwavering confidence that you can pay all your bills each month with ease?
- An abundance of free time to spend with your children or loved ones?
- The weightlessness of being debt free?
- To generously give to others in need?

When you look at what you truly want from your money, what emerges are your underlying values. It becomes more than just the physical dollar bills, or the number reported in your bank account, much, *much* more. It's about living your life in alignment with the values that you hold dear. When money is being spent on experiences, or items that support and align with your goals, it feels good. You are light and breezy, and your heart lifts knowing that money has made possible exactly what you desire. On the flipside, when you find yourself eating out for the fifth time this week, it's not just those extra calories you ate weighing on you, but you also may be carrying a heavy spending hangover.

If you stress about your purchasing habits, or feel regret or guilt over money spent, this could indicate you aren't spending in alignment with your values. For instance, if you love adventure, but a large portion of your paycheck goes toward your growing collection of shoes, you may not be in alignment. But if you instead book a dream vacation to somewhere new, you'll likely feel fabulous and have no remorse over the expense. That's because you're in alignment with your values and money is the tool making it all possible.

I recently spent time going through all my purchases for the entire year, to make sure I had captured all my business expenses. That's the joy of tax time when you're self-employed. I know there are probably easier means to do this by staying on top of it throughout the year (so please don't judge), but the exercise turned out to be rather enlightening. As I looked through the rows and rows of transactions, there were a few items that stood out and had me feeling pretty crappy about my spending.

First off, I could have bought a McDonald's franchise with the amount of money I spent there. And apparently there's no such thing as going to the mall to get "just one thing" in my world. I noticed a trend of at least five purchases for each shopping trip as I sifted through the transactions. What starts out as a mission solely to get my kiddo another pair of new shoes because her feet grow so darned fast turns into a stop at the toy store, a bite to eat at the food court, followed by a sweet treat (can't resist), and of course I have to stop by the book store, where Ivy scolds me to "finish reading the books I already have first."

My attention is drawn to these expenses and I have a visceral reaction because they seem wasteful to me. They aren't aligned with what I value most. I value achievement, adventure, family, and freedom. And although I do also value learning through books, Ivy is right—I have a library at home that I should work on first before adding to the collection. Throughout the list of transactions there are other purchases of course, and some much bigger-ticket items that you would think would garner more attention than my $18 McDonalds drive by. But I don't feel negative or have buyer's remorse when it comes to spending money on the things that I truly value.

I spent money on courses I took throughout the year, and I've spent a good deal of money on my education in general, but I don't think of that as wasteful by any means. I feel proud about those because life-long learning and self-development are so important to me. I spent money on a few trips; Ivy and I went to Mexico and California, and there's no shame when recording those bigger ticket items either because I value adventure, and giving my daughter new places to explore has always been a dream of mine.

Money is nothing in itself. Instead it's the tool that makes the goals and experiences a reality. It made it possible for me to accomplish a major life achievement of mine, to earn my MBA, and to buy my new home. It also enabled me to swim with dolphins with Ivy this year. The accomplishment and the experiences are what matter, and what stands out in our memories, not the money itself. When you can look at money in this light your entire soul fills up with sunshine, as you become the real life version of those ecstatic people in the lottery commercials. It feels so natural and right when money is working in alignment with your true underlying wishes.

Can you think of a recent purchase that you regret? I get it; it happens to all of us. Life is busy and it's easy to get caught up in the day to day of your routine and spend money at each stop, tapping away with those cards, not giving much thought to where it's going. Understanding your values and how you'd like to intentionally spend money takes work and some digging below the surface. But the payoff is so worth it.

When Hannah first met with me a few years ago she was adamant about being able to retire "very soon." When I asked at what age she had in mind, her response was "yesterday." Clearly, she really, *really* wanted to retire, and the sooner the better.

We reviewed her finances and took an inventory of where she stood. She was doing well for herself financially, but based on what she hoped to spend each year during retirement, she didn't quite have enough. She was forty-eight years old, so by no means was she behind others her age. From her shrug at this news, it was clear her comment about being able to retire yesterday was a bit of an exaggeration in fun. But something made her ask. So I inquired further.

I asked her if I could wave my magic wand and make her financially ready and retired tomorrow, what would she be doing?

Her eyes widened and a sly smile appeared across her face. It was as if I had sent Ivy into a candy store with no restrictions. The flood gates opened and she listed all the things she would do including going for lunch with her girlfriends during a weekday with cocktails, having a full spa day with nails and hairstyling, taking a road trip with her daughter to the mountains, joining her mother for a day of playing cards with her ladies club, getting to relax in her outdoor hanging chair with the stack of books she's been wanting to read, and going on a girls trip to Bali.

It all sounded amazing, but I was a tad perplexed as she listed off all the things she wanted to be doing because they all sounded like things she could be doing right now. She made a good income as the lead of human resources at her firm, so I was confused as to why she couldn't incorporate this list into her schedule.

"Why wait until retirement?"

"I should be focused on saving my money at this stage of life, plus I wouldn't have the time," she said.

As she elaborated even further, it turns out she started getting very diligent about saving over these last few years now that her daughter was all grown up and no longer financially dependent on her. Hannah had been a single parent for fifteen years and suspected she had a lot of catching up to do as a single income earner. She was now saving 25% of her income, and found herself working overtime and not taking vacation days in hopes her efforts would be rewarded come bonus time to add even more to her savings.

I could see why she so desperately wanted to retire as of yesterday. She was on track to burn herself out.

Where she was directing her money was not fully aligned with her present values. Don't get me wrong; she was being an ultra-diligent saver, which of course is what us money people like to see. But her super saving strategy was encroaching upon her present happiness level.

We spent some time discussing the things that she wanted to be doing and worked together to identify some of the values underlying the retirement dreams she listed. We identified freedom, flexibility, adventure, relaxation, and family time as the values that lit her up, and the things she wouldn't feel guilty about spending money on.

She absolutely could start doing the activities she dreamed of in retirement, right now. The ones that were in true alignment with her values. But I wanted to show her the proof in the numbers.

After completing her wealth snapshot and Prosperity Plan (which is what she named her forward-looking budget) I provided a complete detailed projection for her to consider with still an early retirement at the age of fifty-seven. Most importantly, it was designed to scale back her current savings rate and free up some cash so she could do the things she was longing to do now.

It took Hannah some time to absorb what she was seeing, and she had lots of follow-up questions. But as the news started to sink in, her shoulders relaxed; a weight was lifted. She was in awe at the opportunity to spend her time doing the things she longed to be doing "one day," *right now*. She didn't have any issues with the work she did; in fact she was passionate about her career. But financial pressure had taken over in recent years, making her lose sight of the elements that she did really enjoy. Knowing she could spend her money on the things she longed to do now along with saving for her upcoming retirement restored a sense of balance.

A couple of months later I was thrilled when I received an email from Hannah, saying she had booked the entire month of July off of work to focus on rest and relaxation. I was so proud that she was embracing her money for what it truly is—a means to achieving her dreams and goals. A quick exit from the workforce wasn't the exact fix she needed at that moment. But allowing herself to use her money now to live in alignment with her values made a huge difference. Her money was there to support her to have more of what she wanted— more relaxation, more freedom and flexibility, more adventure, and more quality time with the people she loved most.

My goal with this book is to get you well acquainted with your money—to make it your thing! But you can see how money is just at the surface, and the things that matter go deeper than the dollar signs. At your core are values that are unique to you and are the driving force of what you want in life and what brings you happiness and joy. If you can get clear on what those values are for you and make sure your money is directed in a way that aligns with them, then you can see money for what it actually is—a tool that can support you to live your best life.

I invite you to spend some time going deeper to identify what you truly want, like Hannah was able to do by uncovering *your* values. Each of you reading this book will have different ones. If you can dig deeper, to find out the value beneath the desire (i.e., "security" or "freedom"), then you can identify what is at the foundation of what you truly want. Knowing what you want makes it clearer when you're using your money in alignment with your values, and when you're not.

Don't get me wrong; there are still going to be instances where you splurge on things or look back on a purchase and wonder why you bought it. And of course there will always be bills to pay that don't exactly feel aligned with your lifelong dreams. But the aim here is to work toward being intentional so that more of your money is directed toward the things and experiences you love, and less is going to what isn't on your bucket list. The more you can do this, the more you'll feel in flow with your financial decisions. That knot in the pit of your stomach will release, and your brain might stop thinking about your savings around the clock. You're in control of your finances, and money is here to support you in living the life of your dreams.

TAKING ACTION

Uncovering Your Values

Imagine you received a windfall of money (this time with no strings attached). Grab a notebook and scrawl out exactly what you would most like to do and/or buy with that money.

Whatever you think of is perfect for this exercise; don't hold back. And no limitations, it's okay if it so happens to include a $300,000 Bentley that you've named Benny. And if your wish list is big, keep it going until you've written down everything your heart desires.

After you've written out everything you would be doing and buying if you had an endless supply of money, now it's time to dig deeper. Reflect on what you wrote and I want you to identify two or three core values that emerge as the theme behind the desire.

If you listed that you want a cottage in nature where your family can come together for every holiday, the values that may emerge from that are family, relaxation, and peace. I've also included a list of values below if you're struggling to put words to the true meaning behind the financial goal.

Keep the list of your values that emerge handy. Write them down somewhere you can easily look back on such as a journal, or you can take a photo of the list so it's easily accessible from your phone. Whatever keeps it top of mind because then you can reread your list of values or have it on hand when you make major financial decisions or big purchases.

Before you proceed on big expenses, equipped with your list you can now ask yourself: does this use of my money align with my values?

Examples of Values

Abundance	Exploration	Innovation	Prosperity
Achievement	Excellence	Inspiring	Purpose
Adventure	Faith	Integrity	Recognition
Authenticity	Fame	Intelligence	Serenity
Balance	Family	Joy	Sharing
Boldness	Fitness	Kindness	Simplicity
Bravery	Focus	Knowledge	Self-development
Calm	Freedom	Leadership	Solitude
Challenge	Friendship	Learning	Spirituality
Charity	Fun	Love	Strength
Comfort	Generosity	Mastery	Success
Community	Gratitude	Meaning	Teamwork
Compassion	Growth	Motivation	Toughness
Confidence	Happiness	Openness	Tranquility
Courage	Hard Work	Optimism	Uniqueness
Creativity	Harmony	Passion	Vision
Curiosity	Health	Peace	Vitality
Enjoyment	Humor	Playfulness	Wealthy
Excitement	Imagination	Positivity	
Experience	Independence	Power	

CHAPTER 16

MONEY *IS* YOUR THING

THERE ARE MANY REASONS you may have felt money isn't your thing before you read this book. It might be because you didn't grow up learning about it, or didn't have much of it, or maybe growing up your parents talked about it negatively. Your reasons may have come later too. Maybe you blew your first real paycheck on a few too many social outings with friends and had to ask your mom to lend you rent money, or maybe saving money always felt out of reach, perhaps just the thought of investing made your head spin, or life got busy and you couldn't find the time.

Wherever you *were* in your relationship with money doesn't matter. Because you read this book, which means you're ready for a change. You're ready to shift from money fear and avoidance to confidence and ease.

Like my client Michelle did. I worked with Michelle for more than five years, and we were set for a quarterly review meeting. She had recently purchased her first home on her own and she was loving it. Her big backyard meant she could finally get the Saint Bernard she had dreamed of because now she had the space to accommodate the puppy that would grow to the size of a person. Not only was the transition perfect for the next stages of her life but she also felt comfortable financially even after all the new expenses that came along with owning versus renting. This was what she was hoping to discuss with me at the meeting—that things were progressing so well overall in her financial life. She'd reached her goals that at one time felt so far out of reach. And now she wanted to make sure there wasn't something that she hadn't given consideration to.

"My money just seems to be on my side for the first time in years," Michelle stated proudly.

"That's awesome!" I cheered.

"But that's what has me a tad confused," Michelle said.

"How so?" I asked.

"There must be more to this, right? Maybe something I'm not getting or something I'm missing? I keep waiting for the other shoe to drop," Michelle said.

Everything was rolling along so smoothly with her money that it all seemed so easy. Perhaps too easy? When Michelle had first started working with me years before, she had no clear plan in place when it came to her finances. When we delved deeper at that first meeting, what stood out as priorities for Michelle were:

- becoming more intentional about saving, to understand if she was putting away enough or needed to increase
- getting started investing, and
- saving for a down payment for a home purchase

We tackled the items one step at a time. We created an individual account that was specifically for savings toward her down payment—to separate it out from her one big slush fund where she'd been putting her savings. We also created a separate account for savings toward her financial freedom and got started investing that portion, as she had a long-term time horizon of at least twenty years for it to grow.

Michelle completed her Magnificent Money Plan (which is the name she chose for her forward-looking budget, which you developed in Chapter 8) and created her saving targets for each category. Then with those amounts in mind, we set up an auto-contribution so her ongoing savings would flow to their specific locations—down payment, surplus account, and financial freedom account.

Michelle had always been a supersaver, so she was comfortable allocating 20% of her gross income as an ultrasound tech between the categories. Of this savings, we calculated that 10% would need to go to her house down payment account, to be ready to purchase a home in four years.

Michelle was motivated by how organized and clear it all became. She no longer felt like she was blindly socking away money without knowing how much she needed and when she would reach her goals. Michelle now knew exactly where her money was going and how much needed to go toward each goal to make them a reality.

Another change that came out of the planning and organizing was how much better she felt about spending money on herself. Previously, anytime she had a night out with her girlfriends, got a massage, or splurged on a touch-up at the salon, she would question the purchases for days and felt bad about spending money. She figured she should probably be saving instead. But when we automated her money to "pay herself first" it assured her that she was indeed doing the work toward her goals. No need to feel guilty. Spending money on herself didn't mean she was taking away from her financial goals or future self because she was already doing that work too.

Fast forward to five years later and Michelle was living in her new home, with lots of space for her soon-to-be-giant doggy. She was now putting away 15% of her gross income into her financial freedom account, since she'd completed the house down payment goal. She loved the idea about being specific with her savings and had started a new account for home expenses to cover any unplanned costs that may arise relating to her new home.

She'd also built an empowerment account that was enough to cover six months' worth of expenses. And based on increases in her salary over the years, her Magnificent Money Plan showed that she could easily spend an additional $350 on discretionary purchases each month without making a dent in her budget.

Michelle continued to be engaged and receptive over the years we worked together. She hit her stride. She was able to check off the boxes for the goals she had already achieved and was making fabulous progress toward her longer-term goals.

Hearing her apprehension about how it all seemed too easy had me smiling wide. It was proof that she had gone from confusion and fear to a woman who had transformed her relationship with her money.

At our check-in meeting, we reviewed where she started and how far she had come.

But it was about more than her getting control of her money. Her entire energy was different. She was open and relaxed as we went through the numbers. She was reassured that she was indeed on track and blown away that it only took a few adjustments and action steps.

in this book who, like you, encountered roadblocks along the way. But power and joy are what lie on the other side of those obstacles, so please don't feel discouraged.

The power of making money your thing comes from taking action. Even small steps can add up to big changes. Building a new habit of saving $25/week when you've been saving nothing up until this point will make a difference to your financial life as it compounds. And the more small actions you take, and changes you make, the easier it all becomes.

You deserve to have money show up in your life as easy. You can and *should* feel confident and empowered about your money. No matter what stage of life you're in or what your level of income, this is possible for everyone. It all begins by choosing to make money your thing.

I made money my thing. Michelle made money her thing. The other women in this book all chose to make money their thing, and now it's your turn.

You've got this.

You're building confidence and feeling empowered about your money.

Because guess what? MONEY IS YOUR THING!